I0500797

The Eleven-Day Week:

A Purification Era

Manos Megalokonomos

Translated from the original greek ENDEKAMERO
by Judith Megas and Patrick Goddard

DORRANCE
PUBLISHING CO
EST. 1920
PITTSBURGH, PENNSYLVANIA 15238

The contents of this work, including, but not limited to, the accuracy of events, people, and places depicted; opinions expressed; permission to use previously published materials included; and any advice given or actions advocated are solely the responsibility of the author, who assumes all liability for said work and indemnifies the publisher against any claims stemming from publication of the work.

All Rights Reserved
Copyright © 2018 by Manos Megalokonomos

No part of this book may be reproduced or transmitted, downloaded, distributed, reverse engineered, or stored in or introduced into any information storage and retrieval system, in any form or by any means, including photocopying and recording, whether electronic or mechanical, now known or hereinafter invented without permission in writing from the publisher.

Dorrance Publishing Co
585 Alpha Drive
Suite 103
Pittsburgh, PA 15238
Visit our website at *www.dorrancebookstore.com*

ISBN: 978-1-4809-8295-6
eISBN: 978-1-4809-8316-8

Table of Contents

1

FLAME DAY

The movement of the air-bus was gentle and smooth despite the fact that all its three floors were packed tight with people. The crush lacked nothing of what had once characterized the old-style, simple buses, when passengers even used to climb onto the roof to ensure themselves a place. For Kamel Aïzentin, however, the day that was beginning was special and he had as yet no cause for complaint, even about the crush, which always annoyed him on his way to work. Of course he was not paying attention to whether anyone was slipping a hand into his pocket to steal his money because there had been no money since the time when he was still a student, let alone a teacher as he was today. The day was special because a new year was starting and he was longing to see the fresh faces of the young children who would join the first class of primary school, brimming with innocent, childish joy, but also a certain apprehension at what this new chapter in their lives held in store. His hand tightened around the sweaty handle of his briefcase. It contained the first item that would leave its mark on this initial scholarly phase of the children's lives.

The temperature had remained high for the eighth month in Alexandria and the sea, nowadays at some distance from the avenue, instead of helping to cool created humidity that weighed on the city's atmosphere night and day. The airbus continued its way towards the centre on its cushion of air, in stark contrast to the wheeled vehicles alongside it with their obsolete technology laboring along the poorly maintained roads.

Kamel's glance lingered only a fraction of a second on the sight of his grandfather's old church, now used as a vegetable market. Also called Kamel, he had been an active, still openly practising Coptic Christian. Under the new circumstances, however, he was forced not to frequent Saint Anthony's Church, though he never stopped declaring himself a Christian. The young Kamel - the teacher now passing in front of the old church – had however been obliged to declare himself an atheist, or, in the current terminology, of "neutral religious persuasion", to have some peace of mind and avoid the difficulties his father had suffered. Indeed, his father, to protect his son, had had Kamel circumcised when still small, as was then the current practice, so that he could if necessary appear a devout Muslim and above suspicion. Nevertheless, Kamel the teacher had a deeply held traditional faith, though he avoided more than a quick glance at the old building where his grandfather used to worship every Sunday. In these times, "Even the walls have ears", as the older generation used to say.

Nearing his destination, the teacher wove his way apologetically through the crush of passengers and at the Greco-Roman Museum stop got off the air-bus. He strode forward, impatient to begin the school year with the first-year pupils who had already arrived at the school with their parents. The school was still affordable, despite the huge economic and other difficulties that people had to deal with in the wake of the disaster that had struck almost all countries of the world in recent years. Parents were still able to bring their children to school with the few things required, and sometimes even a snack.

After the enormous hardships that had befallen people over recent decades, they did not complain. He himself had no complaints despite

2

being, like everyone else, a 'hired' teacher and having managed to work for only five of the eleven years since graduation. He knew fellow ex-students who had worked for less than two years over the same period. He cheerfully entered the building and looked around. The playground was filled with children of all ages accompanied by their parents, and two or three teachers who had already arrived. He hurried to his desk to leave his briefcase, and glanced out of habit at the electronic board: it showed 01/08/2071.

He returned to the playground just in time for the children's allocation to their classes. Later, once back in his classroom, he opened the briefcase and placed the "Logic" (logismic identity) cards on his desk. These were the cards introduced by the "Triptych System" - as the global Inter-Government had deemed it should be called. The cards followed every citizen in the System from the time he or she began the first class of primary school until the time of their death. They had multiple functions and it was forbidden for citizens not to have them to hand, even when asleep. In fact, the greatest distance that a card-holder was allowed from his or her "Logic" card, for the duration or his or her life, was one yard. If this law were broken, an alarm sounded at the local security centre and a "Defender" would immediately appear whose duty was to maintain order. If this breach was intentional and unjustified, the card-holder would be subjected to the implantation of an (RFID) electronic tracker, the cost of which the card-holder was obliged to pay back in installments deducted from his or her income.

As Kamel arranged the "Logic" cards in alphabetical order, he remembered what he had heard when they were handed to him. These cards were far more sophisticated than those in general circulation and of which he himself was a holder. Apart from their other functions, they possessed an educational character. They were programmed to teach pupils on days when they were not attending school. Over-population had obliged the authorities to limit school attendance to five days out of the eleven. In this way, part of the teaching would now take

3

place while pupils were asleep. Kamel already knew this, it had happened with the old cards too, but for a different purpose. The "Triptych System", following the tragedies and disasters that had battered the world over the past fifty years, had focused on its primary duty to protect it from the dangerous obsessions of various fanatics, sometimes as political ideologies and at other times as religious fixations. In this way, in order to neutralize ideas provoked by confrontations between subjects and to achieve control over them, the "Logic" cards operated continuously, even during sleep, exercising an enforced persuasion on the brain. The prolonged repetition of the common- place aspects of behavior required for the maintenance of peace and smooth running of the economy had gradually created a complete mental reformation, facilitating thought control by the authorities. The "Logic" cards had been enhanced by systems supporting many other functions, something that Kamel suspected but had no way of confirming. He only knew that billions of files relating to the location of each "Logic" card and its holder throughout the world were registered and stored at all times at the Central Security Service. Thus the CSS was compiling a database containing all details, giving the "System" the capability to hold information concerning exactly where each "Logic" card was at any given moment; also, that is, about where and when each of the billions of subjects who held the cards were, in order – according to the CSS – for prompt attention to be paid to everyone's security. The requisite electronic material had in any case already been prepared way back in the first decade of the 21st century: technology had then entered people's lives at great speed, with the ultimate goal of familiarizing them to such an extent that they would tolerate, as was said, even an analogous bodily implant, to enable the greatest possible continuity of surveillance by the authorities.

"No one," thought Kamel, "had attached any importance to this development, neither had the apt words of one of the Founding Fathers of the United States, Benjamin Franklin, been remembered, that 'Whoever gives up essential liberty to obtain a little temporary safety deserves neither of the two.'"

With these thoughts in mind, he heard the happy voices of the children in the corridor as they arrived to enter the classroom and sit at their desks for the first time, "....and for the first time to be connected to the "Logic" cards that will accompany them for the rest of their lives", thought Kamel, "..delivering them up to the tight embrace of the rest of society and the System".

• • •

"After a demonic storm will come the divine sunshine..." Michos could not remember where he had read this. It haunted him every evening and his every dream contained some reminder of it. In any case, he did not sleep well, what with the almost daily travelling, the long distances, and the different people he had to meet to talk over and agree upon the disposition of the products he sold in the markets. "...After a demonic storm will come the divine sunshine". "Enough of the demonic storm! Before you go to sleep, think about what you've got done and what there is left to do tomorrow." Tomorrow.... was perhaps the most important day, not for his work but for himself. For years he had been waiting for chance to bring him to this strange place because he couldn't travel wherever he wanted. The times would not allow it. His work was demanding and every hour counted to accumulate the "points" that every worker needed – and not just for him, whose present job was serious and well-paid. Points were what every worker needed to keep active and not sink into obscurity and hunger. *Tomorrow! Tomorrow, I'll be able to face myself. Who I am and who the other Michos was, or Michalis to be precise. My grandfather, the eminent scientist who left me this note and who hid, here, near the hotel where I'm now going to sleep, his research notes, his invention. The research which then, at the beginning of the twenty first century, was considered so dangerous. So dangerous that its creator was forced not only to then bury it but also to deny its very existence".

It was pure chance that the younger Michos had found himself with an expertise that bore some relation to his grandfather's work.

His job was to sell the pharmaceutical products which enabled people to refrain from violence, to treat themselves for depression - the commonest global health problem now that malnutrition was considered a social symptom rather than a treatable condition - and, above all, to deter suicide. In fact, as Michos suspected, these drugs were also a means not only to discourage the population from any form of resistance, but also to strongly influence, via the "Triptych System", their personal lives - if, that is, one accepted that today there still remained anything which could be considered a personal life. Thus for this medication there were strict instructions from on high. Instructions for it to be supplied at a low cost to users and the pharmaceutical companies to retain only one third of the profits customarily made from other medicines. This antidepressant formulation was a kind of sequel to the anti-terrorism medication which had been in circulation fifteen years before to eradicate all fears arising from external threats. Its purpose was to create billions of credit modules for the pharmaceutical companies, but also to keep the populations in a submissive, semi-hypnotic state which would preclude any resistance to the decisions of Authority. For this reason, any refusal to take this "necessary" medication was considered a serious crime. Generally, production and distribution of medicines were at such a high level globally that they compared only with the activity of those companies specializing in the maintenance of the "Triptych System" and the production and disposition of its defenders.

He glanced again at the book which he hoped would lead him to the discovery of his grandfather's research.

"Manas" was its title, "The Heroic Epic of Kyrgyzstan". It was a long epic, longer than any other that Michos had seen. Longer than the "Odyssey" and the "Iliad", longer than the Indian "Mahabharata"...It was the history of Manas, the hero of the region. He had lived at some unspecified time around one thousand to one thousand one hundred years ago, when Islam had not yet prevailed in the region and the memory of the Amazons was still very much alive. Michos had not managed to read the whole epic. However, he knew that certain lines were directly related to the place where the notes on his grandfather's findings had been hidden. The largest monument to Manas was in the city of Bishkek. This was where Michos had just arrived, believing that the book together with the monument would give him the solution to the problem preoccupying him. He once more took the note from the former Mihalis. He had learned it almost word for word but something told him that in there was a phrase that would shed light on what he was seeking.

"My dear Yiorgos,"

his grandfather had written to the younger Michos's father,

"At this advanced age, I don't know yet whether the reward I have been fated to receive for my work is a blessing or a curse. It concerns the discovery which, when I announced it at the French Academy a few months ago, created an uproar with every population of the world willing to move heaven and earth - some in order to obtain it no matter what, others to hinder its application. The reason being that it was considered so revolutionary, so subversive that its consequences for the future were thought by some to be beneficial and by others catastrophic: beneficial or catastrophic both for human cognition and for the spiritual well being of society as a whole. I have lived my entire life based on one principle: the Socratic maxim, "If it were necessary for me to do wrong or be wronged, I would prefer to be wronged rather than do wrong." Thus, with a heavy heart I have taken the decision to conceal my discovery and make a second announcement to the academics: that there was an oversight in the theory upon which I had relied; an oversight that has made my work ineffective and basically valueless. Something, I confess to you alone, which is not true. It is a fact that a great many threats were made against me by various centres of power as well as by para-governmental agents who tried to obtain details of my work from me, and this contributed to my decision.

It is by chance that I find myself in the capital of Kyrgyzstan today, the day when I have taken this decision, and I understand that I have no time to lose. My pursuers are only one step behind me. My secret may become terrifyingly

7

dangerous, I repeat, if it falls into the wrong hands. Handling it requires great care. I give you below the clues that can put you on the right path to find the dossier containing all the technical details of my work. Details that, as far as I know, you are capable of decoding. These are: the number 12, the sword of the national hero of Kyrgyzstan and the numbers 13492 and 13493.

May you succeed, my dear son."

The fading text seemed to burn his hands. As if his antecedent had returned to life and was urging him to rise to the challenge of the secret entrusted to him. Michos felt the blood rising to his head and struggled to control himself. This was not a good moment for his "Logic" card to register palpitations. He was well aware that every change in the functioning of his body was being recorded by that mandatory appendage and every piece of information, like a cardiograph, would be conveyed automatically to the control centre, no matter where its source might be. It was no longer possible for an individual-citizen to hide so much as an illness or a simple worry from the System.

Michos continued staring at the letter he had just read. Yiorgos, his father, had never had the opportunity to travel and certainly never so far from Greece. He had simply spent a few years as a migrant worker in northern Europe after the catastrophe that had befallen his homeland, which had lasted until the forties. He had lived through the upheavals both as a child at the time of the brief but ruinous clashes referred to as the "Petrol Wars" and later, as a mature man, when wars had been waged in the name of water. As long as he had remained in Greece, the widespread poverty and economic pressures created conditions that made every sort of expenditure or even ideas that were not directly related to pure survival out of reach for himself, his wife and his son. Michos' father, Yiorgos, had not managed to achieve the same comfortable position in society as the older Mihalis. Studies were out of the question. Food and accommodation were the first requirements. He finally returned, as did many others, to a smallholding he had inherited and lived together with his family producing the fruit and vegetables still needed by the markets after the breakup of the European Union. He was at least able to afford an education for Michos, who was now holding the old, handwritten page containing his grandfather's obscure riddle.

· · ·

"That's the first day of school over", thought Kamel as he relaxed. "There are many more to come, but it's the first that gives a foretaste of what lies ahead". The day had gone well. The children were content, especially with the handing out of the "Logic" cards, when they found that apart from the teaching material contained in them, there were games for them to play when not busy with homework.

"That's the first day over", thought Kamel, yet he realized from several indications that, as was the case almost every year now, the "Logic" cards he had distributed had again certain differences from the previous year. Kamel thought of the many things that had happened when he began teaching several years ago.

It was the period following the wars generally referred to as the Petrol Wars and the Water Wars. Basically, these were not prolonged wars like those of the twentieth century, but brief, regional clashes involving the intervention of the great powers and multinational corporations that brought order to local disputes to serve their own interests. It was only after these conflicts that the central power of the "Triptych System" had been formed consisting of those countries that then constituted the Great Powers together with international business giants and the banking interests they represented. Naturally, the system also included the old state powers represented by their own "commissars", whose power was however nominal and their presence only necessary in order for them to convey to the populations of once independent nation states the directives of the "Triptych System" that every regional legal system had to follow. Legislation had passed almost entirely to the global "Triptych" and its categorization of citizens had defined three "Castes" with specific remuneration for each. In credit units they represented 10,000 for the golden caste, 1,000 for the silver caste and 100 for the bronze.

Hence the globalization that began in the last decades of the twentieth century had acquired its final form. Together with this outcome a kind of peace was assured since social unrest had disappeared. Kamel remembered how this effort to impose peace had begun. Efforts, mostly by the Americans to impose 'democracy' proved to be a utopic idea and had failed. The spread of Islam in the west had prevented this effort and resulted in small-scale conflicts, since for many years the population of Europe had been mainly Muslim. Thus, in order to stop the religious rivalry that had frequently broken out with particularly bloody clashes, a series of measures were introduced; these included heavy fines for challenging the authority of the police, or for wearing clothing that concealed the face at demonstrations, and the imposition of harsh punishments for unauthorized demonstrations. The freedoms and rights of citizens were incompatible, according to the legislation of the "System", with the survival of globalization and had to be quietly and gradually abolished. Of course, previous references to laws related to challenging the authority of the police were now replaced by the concept of total subjugation to their substitutes, the Defenders of the international system.

The consequences of globalization were not only geo-political, but extended to economic, social and political spheres. Many important changes, modifications and mutations took place. Among others, the traditional sphere of anarchy at the end of the twentieth century, whose undisputed aim was the anti-establishment struggle, was supplanted by moves, accepted by the peoples and others under appropriate aliases, leading to the decline of homelands and the rise of cosmopolitanism. A multicultural and ethnically amorphous society was absolutely necessary in order to achieve complete globalization and the huge wealth of the colossal international corporations.

His "Logic" card interrupted the thoughts occupying him. It had been activated by his wife's card and was showing a picture. It was a picture that he had secretly hoped never to see. His wife, upon opening the front door, had been faced with what every citizen feared. A defender. A short and robot-like, mechanical creature with a hexagonal head, two cold, yellow eyes, a third different, red eye and a square mouth which opened and closed as it spoke; its appearance did not bode well. His wife Nora looked terrified. She had not however activated the sound for Kamel to hear what was said. Unable to react in any other way, he raced out of the classroom into the street and began searching for some means of getting home as quickly as possible. A visit to whatever house from a defender was always bad news.

• • •

The monument to Manas has been erected on a marble base about seven metres high. The actual statue is a further three metres in height and represents the Hero astride his horse at full gallop, his sword grasped in his outstretched hand to the right, as if in eternal battle. A battle against the enemies of his nation, a nation which did not exist anymore. "It's a wonder such a nationalistic symbol has survived so many decades without having been neglected, ridiculed or demolished", thinks Michos as he stands at a distance to study the face, since only from some distance can one see the face of the Hero at such a height. "In my country they would have destroyed it, ridiculing all those whose happiness depended on any, even iconic, idea of independence."

Michos tries to calculate the distance with his eye. In the message he left, his grandfather refers to at least two details that he understands: the sword and the number twelve. If we assume that the number refers to the height of the sword from the ground in metres, the answer must be under the stone covering the ground space. Yet it was obviously impossible to hide anything there. "If the number," thinks Michos, "refers to the distance in the direction indicated by the Hero's sword......Alright, in that direction there is a smaller statue on a smaller base. Michos approaches, but the name of the person represented by the smaller statue has long been obliterated by age, grime and the harsh climate. In any case, Michos can see no spot which can be used as a hiding place for his spiritual legacy. He cannot see how the other five digit numbers on the message relate to the details he has. Michos spends some time walking around the statue as well as the building – of modern design for the twentieth century – which is close by, but no detail gives him anything to help in his search.

Back in the hotel, he tries to order his thoughts and he re-reads his grandfather's message. He feels a growing emptiness as hope of the discovery he has waited for all his life begins to fade. When he feels disappointment for any reason, he is in the habit of returning to his happiest moment. It is not a simple consolation for him. He always sees it and relives it as if it is taking place in the present. *"Because I want to live it as if it were today. I am in that fashion house"* he recalls, *"on the orders of the company to study any possibility for us to take on medicine distribution. Initially, I didn't fully understand the purpose. But when the fashion show starts and I see the mannequins parading in front of me with their familiar, professional swaying gait, I begin to understand. It was obvious that the slim, almost fleshless girls need some sort of support – medical or simply pharmaceutical, I don't know – to recover from their anorexia nervosa, an almost general condition in their profession. Their elbows, knees and hips give the impression with every swaying step of trying to break free and escape from their covering of skin, while their facial expressions are almost always unhappy, consistent with the feigned seriousness which they try to present. This is what I see and I am meditating on how I can handle this commercial-medical problem in the interest of the Company, when I notice something different: the light. An unexpected glow. A woman who is illuminating all around her, a woman who looks like a real woman, with the poise that in itself attracts admiration, the gaze that meets my gaze and the walk which falters almost but not quite imperceptibly, as if she wants to re-*

tain my admiration for a thousandth of a second. The vision passes and I remain stunned by its impact. I wait and hope that she will pass again wearing a different dress – not having of course any recollection of the first. She passes me again and again, and each time I discern that hesitation, the split second delay in her step which shows something different, the invisible, our personal aura. I wait outside the fashion house after the show and as she comes out, I approach her without a qualm. I know that she is with me. She also knows it. That is the story of my happiest moment. For as long as it lasts. For as long as it lasted."

Michos' happiness lasted for a year. Alison was then twenty and Michos just turned thirty. Their lives were before them and every moment was limitless pleasure. It was happiness that could not be lost. However, at the end of the year there was the great reform. Three castes were designated, each citizen assumed the position assigned to him or her by the system. Michos remained in his job but Alison was obliged to leave and carry out other duties. The continuation of their love was forbidden. Their separation was both sad and painful. Over the ten years since then, Michos had had no other relationship, he had not wanted one, he had no thought of marriage. He remained alone. With one name, one memory. "One name", he is thinking now in the hotel in Bishkek. "One name is missing". He realizes that there is a gap in his thoughts. The name lying under the age-old grime of the second statue, the one standing twelve metres away from the blade of Manas' sword.

"I have to get some rest, tomorrow is a difficult day", he is thinking, but calming down is easier said than done. "The opportunity to uncover grandfather's secret is not likely to present itself again. What's more, my delay tomorrow will be noted by central surveillance. But I've thought about Alison again, haven't I? It is a ridiculous situation for a mature man with so much experience to feel disturbed by a woman he separated from ten years ago."

But the truth was that it happened every time he thought about her. He had often considered replacing her, if not in his thoughts and his heart, at least with another physical relationship. And he had made two or three attempts which, however, had only lasted a few days. The presence of those women and their contact with him had been just enough to remind him, even more vividly, of the woman he had loved; to make her absence even more intense; to give rise to comparisons that played havoc with his equilibrium. Hence, he had abandoned his efforts some time ago. He had even considered replacing the female presence with one of the special imitation robots that were in circulation and whose company one could obtain for a few or for many hours simply by sending a message. People he knew who had tried this solution had confirmed that the way the robots operated was only slightly different from a real woman with a real woman and the techniques they used had certainly far greater variety than those a normal lover could offer. But he had not resorted to this solution. He was, he concluded, among the few of his contemporaries who persisted in antiquated ideas and behaviour patterns as was obvious simply from the fact that he was still in love with the woman he had lost ten years ago. Since their separation, there had been very few occasions when he had learned that Alison was somewhere or that he was somehow in her thoughts. He had received a few rare messages from her, on occasions that he was unable to determine the nature of. On days and at times not related either with her name day or with her birthday – celebrations which anyway had lost all meaning with the new system's culture – not even their own common experiences, the important dates or unforgettable moments they had lived together. Her very few messages - fewer than one a year - had nothing in common with each other. As if she were following a plan of her own, derived from her present life and quite unknown to him. As if with these messages she were seeking to provide some sort of support, not for him but rather to confirm something for herself, for her to support herself at a difficult moment. "What is she doing, how and where is she living, why did they take her away from me, how does she spend her time?" Michos had never ceased to wonder.

2

DUMBDAY

The square dedicated to the hero, Manas, was heavy with the previous night's humidity and the dawn mist lay inert under the heavy air. The hero was clear to see from the legs of the horse and above, while the base of the statue was only just visible as Michos approached. Fortunately, the square was still deserted since he wanted to be alone while he searched for the name he needed. He had brought a large sponge with him from the bathroom in the hotel and began to scrub the pedestal of the statue standing twelve metres away from that of Manas. It was certain to create problems for his plans if some defender were to appear or a camera were to record his strange activity. But the sponge quickly uncovered a woman's name. It must have been a name associated with the country's history, but definitely unknown to him. Before he could feel disappointment, however, the sponge uncovered another word, roughly carved into the marble like the graffiti scrawled by youngsters on public monuments. "Carved" was an exaggeration. It had been scratched hurriedly and crudely alongside the original name of the woman. More cleaning revealed letters that made some sense. The hurried engraver had written the word AMAZONA in capital letters. "Had it been written without the final A, anyone might have written it," thought Michos instinctively. But that final A showed that it could have been written by a Greek hand and, why not, perhaps even by the elder Mihalis. He turned quickly and began the walk back before some passerby should notice him. By the time he got to the hotel, a thought had struck him: "How much simpler everything had been when people still had a personal life". Before a person felt that his every thought was controlled by an external and constraining surveillance. Before the "Triptych System" did away with all protection of what was once known as "personal data". And this had come about through an effort to deter brutal acts of terrorists and religious fundamentalists who had been the scourge of the forties and fifties.

"So, Amazona," he thought as he opened his grandfather Mihalis' electronic memory in his "Logic" card. The one good thing about "Logic" cards was that no one needed any other electronic device to do any sort of work, to communicate or conduct a search. Everything was stored in the memory of every foundation, service or library. One could communicate with any part of the world, find any person one wished to communicate with, type a message and send a document, hear the official instructions of the system and receive indication of any possible warning concerning an oversight or irregularity. Of course, the system always knew exactly where on the planet any cardholder could be found and what he or she was up to, as well as what he or she was saying and whom he or she was communicating with, since the card was never further than one yard away from its holder.

The screen projected onto the wall of his room by the "Logic" card told him the following: "On the borders of Kazakhstan, in the city of Pakrova, during archeological excavations seventy years ago, a series of fifty tholos tombs were unearthed dating from the 4th century BC. Next to the female skeletons, they found typical symbols of status: necklaces, sacred stones and objects used in religious rituals. Many of these skeletons had bowed shin bones, characteristic of "professional" horse riders. Moreover, skeletons of babies were only found with the male skeletons. Not a single one was found buried next to a female. All these discoveries clearly indicated that warfare belonged among women's occupations while the rearing of children was exclusively men's work."

Michos kept the name of the town for future reference and requested the C.E.M. (Central Electronic Memory) give him the names of Amazons from antiquity. Immediately, names both known and unknown to him began to appear, mainly those from pre-historic times, thought to have been killed fighting for Troy, but also others from different periods. Names like Hippolyte, Kloni, Myrini, Penthesilea, Antiopeia, Deianeira, Thatestris, Polemousa, Antandre, Armotheir, Hippothoe and many others brought something to mind, but continued to remain completely unknown to him. None had any connection with what he knew about his grandfather Mihalis' work. He stopped searching when he realized that he was only wasting time. He decided instead to search his grandfather's files; perhaps there he would find something that reminded him of one of the names just obtained from the Memory. He found none that related to the electronic folders. He then began to open his grandfather's folders one by one and search every title and chapter for one of the names from the Memory. The day wore on and he felt more and more anxious. By now, after so many hours, it would be impossible for the delay in his work schedule to go unnoticed by his company's central office. He picked up the old text of "Manas" and read the two lines, numbers 13492-13493, that matched the numbers in his grandfather's letter. The lines described a clash between the hero and a woman. A female warrior, Rabiginga.

"The hero rushed at her knife
And thus it pierced his arm".

It was clear that this referred to a woman likened by the epic to the ancient Amazons. Immediately the idea came to him. Many more recent narratives equated other women with Amazons, apart from those of the Trojan War and the time of Alexander the Great. There were, for example, those that had fought against the Spanish conquistadors in the Amazon. He searched and found that, while exploring Brazil in 1542 with a party of Spanish soldiers, Francisco de Orelleana was confronted by something astonishing. On the banks of a river, he was surrounded by a party of warriors whose leader was a stunningly beautiful woman. "She was tall, muscular and impetuous, and the only clothing she wore was a scrap of cloth". This was how she was described by Gaspar de Carvajal, the mission's chronicler. According to one version, it was this encounter that had prompted the Spaniards to give the name Amazon to the great river. There were other cases, too, in which references were made to Amazon warrior-women in still more recent times....

Michos again picked up the "Logic" card and put in a search for the names of women considered to be Amazons in more recent stories. The first to appear was a name that seemed familiar: "Maximo". He had seen it mentioned in his grandfather's files but had read it as "Maxímos", the name of a certain important intellectual and politician from more recent Greek history. He now saw that Maximo, on the other hand, was an Amazon well-known for her actions in the Middle Ages, actions that had brought her into confrontation with Digenis Akritas. They ended up fighting and naturally Digenis won. Maximo, according to the file, asked him to have intercourse with her. She had sworn herself to eternal virginity unless she were to suffer a 'crushing defeat' at the hands of a man, according to the old poems. In conclusion, the legend recounted how Digenis at first refused but finally gave in to the persuasive words and beauty of the Amazon because, wrote the poet, "She was young and good, beautiful and a virgin".

Michos turned back to the files. He tried to open the "Maximo" file but found that opening it required a double password. The key word that had been valid for the other files would not open "Maximo".

"13492, 13493", thought Michos. He tapped in the numbers but without result. He then began to insert, letter by letter, the two lines which contained the description of Manas' confrontation with his Amazon, Rabiginga, and the entire folder opened as if by magic. He was now extremely excited. Neither the delay in his schedule nor the dangers this represented could distract him from the screen on the wall lit up by the "Logic" card.

But then something else attracted his attention. He had a message from Alison. It was different from the random, brief to the point of indifferent messages he received from time to time, like "Happy Christmas" or "Many happy returns". This one was by far the most inexplicable. It didn't contain anything. No text at all. Just a signature: "Alison".

• • •

Kamel had never expected to find himself so far from his home city of Alexandria, to be travelling in this air-car in the hope of finding his wife and children. As soon as he was informed of the Defender's visit to his home, he had tried to communicate with his family but not one of their three "Logic" cards was working. He ran along the old coastal road, the Corniche, as if afflicted by some virus of insanity. He realised that the sight of a grown man running through the calm crowds of pedestrians was not something that would go unnoticed. Society had become addicted to the serenity of total security guaranteed by the Triptych System and its continuous presence. There had been many crises over the previous decades. These crises had spawned a global government, a single monetary system and a powerful administrative oligarchy. An oligarchy supported by a handful of super-corporations, created by the collapse of the majority of multinational companies.

These, together with the creation of an international police force, an international army and Legal system had eliminated the fear of terrorism for people of the late twenty first century.

Despite all the resulting restrictions for the average citizen and the absence of any suggestion of democracy, for nearly ten years now a sense of security had for the first time been created for every member of the global system. Hence, since the creation of the Triptych System, people no longer felt endangered by acts of terrorism, a fear felt by the whole of society up until the middle of the century.

For these reasons the sight of a man running as if insane in the calm atmosphere of the city that afternoon would be completely unexpected. Kamel had arrived home to find neither his wife nor his two children. The neighbours he asked could not, or did not want to give him any information about his family and he had been obliged to send a message via his "Logic" card to the local Defender station. He was requested to go to the station to receive the relevant information. This answer was rather unusual, thought Kamel, since the Defenders were not known to communicate directly with citizens. All procedures took place via the "Logic" cards and were carried out through impersonal questions and answers and stilted instructions. The reason for this exception was very clear to Kamel when he arrived at the Defenders station, where an officer, surrounded by his three mechanical colleagues, explained that the family had been taken to a place for reformation and regeneration, to protect them from the danger of religious proselytizing, something which his wife Nora had been detected doing.

Kamel's next moves were an unbelievable nightmare. It did not cross his mind to question the officer's assertion. That would have been pointless, as much as he believed adamantly that Nora could not possibly have done something not only illegal but also stupid. They had lived together through the whole period when adherence to the old religions had begun to create endless problems and catastrophic conflicts. Together they had also experienced the entire campaign and the activities aimed at the neutralizing of religions, not only to put a stop to the massacres but also to control thought for the purpose of world peace. Kamel and Nora had closely followed the relevant compulsory lessons. These were entitled: "The three stages for thought control" and were aimed at peace between communities that had hitherto been massacring each other indiscriminately. They contained a type of what used to be referred to as "brainwashing", through the extended repetition of commonplace tasks, intense vilification of religious people as paranoid and patriots as fanatical and dangerous nationalists, sleep deprivation, compulsory attendance of lessons and night time viewing of television programmes featuring intensely emotive scenes. The second phase was characterized by cognitively empty intervals involving techniques such as hypnosis interspersed with continual announcements about the reforms, making it impossible for the audience to compare their futures with their past lives. The third phase consisted of enforced persuasion on the necessity of certain administrative and practical measures relating to everyday life. Proselytizing was among the first and main activities to be forbidden, as this was considered the principal cause of the fanaticism of the past. The idea that Nora had tried to convert anyone seemed absurd to Kamel as he entered the air-car that would take him from the El Hantra el Bacharia station to the detention camp at Lake Issyk Koul in Central Asia. This was where they had taken Nora and his children.

• • •

All Kamel could hear was a whistling sound as the air-car covered the distance between North Africa and Central Asia at speeds of over five hundred kilometers an hour. He had already passed over Asia Minor and the Caspian Sea. To right and left, Kamel saw the permanently snow-covered slopes of the Altai Mountains passing like towering white walls. The speed was such that one imagined the air-car would hit the rocky surface at any second, but at the last moment it always veered and passed close by – as if by magic.

The air-car's twists and turns at one point forced Kamel to grasp his "Logic" card to prevent it sliding away from him and obliging him to apologise to the control centre. He always regarded his card with mixed emotions: sometimes with total devotion and sometimes with total hatred. The hatred stemmed from the first time realised that he would never experience anything without it passing through central surveillance for analysis. That he would never be further than one yard from this continuous supervision. However, he also regarded it with the respect he would have had for a faithful body- guard, since it was thanks to the card that no danger could threaten him, no matter where he was or what he did, in contrast to the continuous fear that his father had experienced in previous decades, fear that the Triptych System had completely eliminated from society as soon as it had gained global dominance. Thus the previous dictatorship of fear which had tyrannized citizens had been replaced by a compulsory, enforced security. As this security established itself, it was evident that an important role had been played by fear itself. This was natural, since its cultivation and dissemination had constituted a vehicle for profit, socio-political influence, propaganda and the manipulation of the public, which had then led to the colossal need for the manufacture and distribution of defenders. It was characteristic of the age how swiftly certain figures had emerged to exploit this fear and, by cultivating it, to create security organizations and businesses to control every social activity. Thus it was gradually accepted as necessary for the survival of everyone, right down to the least significant of citizens.

Beyond the security question, however, the "Logic" card had helped Kamel to become one of the most knowledgeable teachers in the field of classical studies. His powerful memory had played an important role. The continuous presence of the card complemented his knowledge and helped him keep in mind the teachings of the numerous ancient and Renaissance philosophers memorised when he was a child. The lack of social advancement that had accompanied his professional career did not especially bother him. Moreover, the fact that he had remained a primary school teacher had left him with more time to enrich himself with the wisdom of the ancients; with knowledge, that is, which had been completely discredited by the social system. This was natural since such knowledge was no longer necessary for the production of wealth - now the only thing required of education in the Age of Purification. This was the name most often used to refer to the end of the twenty first century. It was also called the "Age of Purification", because it followed those first decades characterized by petrol wars, by water wars, by a horrifying nuclear catastrophe in Asia and, finally, by savage conflicts and massacres of populations in Europe and Asia on the pretext of religious differences. "Purification Camp" was in any case the name for the place where the defenders had taken Nora and the children. Where Kamel was now going, determined to share in his family's fate. His only consolation was that this camp, according to the officer at the Alexandria station, was a category "A" camp. That is, it belonged to the category where subjects were taken who had committed less serious misdemeanors. The other categories were "B", which received those who had committed serious crimes, and "C" from which, it was rumoured, inmates were never released alive. The security industry that had developed in the wake of the religious conflicts tolerated no leniency. Kamel stepped out at the stop on the north slopes of a huge mountain range at an altitude of 1600 metres. A gust of wind hit him in the face as he headed towards the sign indicating transport to Purification Camp Number 425. As he walked to the side of the road, he sensed a sheer drop deep in the near darkness and saw, far away, lights glittering, reflected on a vast surface of water. It was, he thought, the famous lake of Issyk Koul, the second highest lake on Earth.

· · ·

A soft, female hand is caressing the fur. It is her own hand, scented with the best "Lamika" product and immaculately manicured. The fingernails are finely filed, curved and unexpectedly transparent - as befits her class. Not simply "A" class, but her more exclusive category within the "A" class. The fingers sink into the fur and produce in her a familiar ripple of pleasure. Of course, the hypnotic substance, glafka, a vapourised drink, which Rasel, the servant of the day, has just directed into her nostrils has helped. Life holds some enjoyment, she is thinking, trying to dispel the catatonic boredom that is her usual companion. How she would like to do something that would give her real pleasure! Something other than the frequent erotic encounters she is free to arrange. Something beyond the unlimited pleasures provided by food. Beyond the new experiences provided by continuous travelling. One of her two permanent partners is obsessed with security, perhaps because he is older and still has vivid memories of that time when no one could move without fear of sudden extermination by the insane people still freely circulating.

That was two decades ago and the few unbalanced people left alive were now confined to specific colonies. They had also been suitably lobotomized so no longer presented a threat to any person or animal, rich or poor, leader or citizen. The idea of a lobotomy, which had been a necessity for that generation, briefly came to her as she buried her manicured fingers in the fur of the leopard's neck. This was only possible because the big cat had undergone, as far as she knew, such an operation. Her other partner had been responsible for this. The harmless leopard had been a gift from him, her first partner having up-staged him with the gift of a floating villa, in which she had travelled constantly for almost the past three endekamera, a whole month. Klara smiled as she sank sweetly into drowsiness and tightened her fingers deep in the colourful fur. The leopard, calm as an old cat, purred languidly.

The fur caressed by Klara was soft, but the handrail gripped by the furious Amsey was hard. Certainly life had never been as easy for her as it had been for Klara. Amsey held the handrail with her eyes fixed on the beautiful view of the island close to which was moored the floating palace of her mistress. It was the very same island. The same reflecting light. The same late summer heat. The same soft ripples on the water between herself and the shoreline. As if so many years had not passed. She even began to imagine that if she turned her gaze to the right, she would see the same beloved figure. Someone just as ready to burst out laughing as to give serious thought to the questions of life. Just as in the past, however, Amsey was unable to defy the System which had ordered that they separate, that she leave him and take up, as she was ordered at the time, the duties programmed for her. "Programmed" was the correct word. It was a vague, impersonal programme put in place with a "click" within the appropriate framework. She had not known then – but it would not have mattered anyway – that the "appropriate framework" was the sphere of beauty and every pleasure for members of the ruling class. Her beauty was enough for such a role. She was, however, also equally qualified to manage complex situations with a profound intelligence. Something which made her much in demand with those in power.

She again tightened her grip on the handrail to stop herself from turning her gaze. It was as if not a moment had passed since that time. Much had taken place during those ten years but nothing had eroded the memory. The love. The happiness. The sudden surge she felt each time her thoughts reunited her with Michos. Her thoughts were anyway always close to him, just as he should have been standing close to her at the rail now, their shoulders touching. But her position in the leadership's aesthetic pleasure sector did not allow the continuation of such a relationship - their relationship. Not only when assigned the role of official concubine to a leading figure in the global economy, but also afterwards. When, as today, she no longer held the position of concubine to the powerful of the Earth but simply cared for another woman, also a concubine now, with the temporary advantage of her youth. Amsey was always to hand, responsible for any mishap, difficulty or complication that might occur between the young woman and the two leaders with whom she shared her bed. Perhaps the fact that Amsey was never able to be with Michos again had helped her keep alive this permanent relationship from a distance. Because he had never been out of her thoughts for even a second. Because not a single day passed without her knowing where he was, whom he was seeing, when he was travelling, even what images passed before his eyes at any given moment. The System gave her the technical capability for this discreet tele-surveillance, but she also had the privileges of Caste A, permitted to her both at the technical and the legal levels. She thought Michos had called her. But, no. He still knew her only as Alison, the Anglo-Saxon name which she had later changed. She had gone back to her traditional Navajo Indian name. At that time, feeling so oppressed by the System crushing her, that would not allow her any control over what she wanted in life - to live her own life, to understand where she belonged - she had returned to her original name of Amsey. At least in that way she knew that she had not integrated, that she had not been completely crushed as the system desired. That she had not completely lost her individuality. That, in spite of her suffering, she had retained her soul untouched with her original name: Morning Mist.

Amsey heard someone calling and understood when she saw Klara's servant behind her. It was the time when Klara used to be entertained by the holograms. She glanced one more time at the island opposite and wondered if it was by pure coincidence that she found herself in this same place where they had been separated; on the day when, after so many years, the fortunes of the man she loved appeared to be entering a dangerous phase. She stifled an unexpected sob – it had been years since she had been like this – and headed for the lift to go down to Klara's personal relaxation area.

Klara received her warmly. She always admired Amsey's aristocratic air and beauty. It was different from her own. Her own blondeness gave her the classic appearance of the glamour girl. Amsey, with her dark, radiant skin, her enormous dark eyes and her noble bearing, made it easy to imagine her riding into battle on a war-horse. Klara was also happy about what was to happen next. Amsey came forward smiling and helped her remove the flimsy nightdress covering her superb body. She then took the leopard by the collar and handed it to Rasel. She indicated he should remove the animal from his mistress's presence. The lobotomy had transformed it into a harmless 'pussycat' but no one knew how the creature might react to the proce-dure about to take place through the physical touch conveying holo-gram. As soon as Rasel left the chamber pulling the leopard along behind him, Amsey put two drops of the hypnotic substance into the water-pipe beside Klara and adjusted the central computer to run her mistress's favourite programme. The computer possessed endless pos-sibilities for showing and conveying a realistic atmosphere ranging from that of a spa town environment, to that of the sea, mountain or jungle. Everything seemed so real that the device's owner would never feel the need to move, let alone travel to places where, infrequently of course, there was always the possibility of being confronted by some danger or other. The programme set up by Amsey for Klara was called the 'Polypus' effect but had nothing to do with what was once thought of as a health problem. On the contrary, this was the ultimate erotic programme.

When she saw the haze enveloping the naked Klara like a cloud, her eyes registering the first smile of anticipation, Amsey gradually increased the intensity of the programme. This had the capability to intensify the hologram, creating the potential for a concrete sensation of touch on the skin and all intimate parts of the body enveloped in the cloud. Klara was already in total ecstasy. The blonde woman was lost in the thickening cloud around her, alone in another world of her own; and in the isolation she now no longer felt alone.

Amsey now had time to think. To think anxiously about whether she had helped or had pushed Michos nearer the edge of the precipice with the message she had sent him a few hours earlier. "I only wanted to help", she found herself saying. "That's all I wanted. And I can't find out if I have done you good or harm. Forgive me." The dread she had forgotten for so long had suddenly risen in her throat to re-mind her that there was indeed something to fear.

• • •

"Many moments, up to a whole lifetime, could be lived between two ticks of a clock, when the clocks still ticked the passing seconds of people's lives," thought Michos. He had in front of him both Alison's brief message and his grandfather's vital computer message. These were two ticks which revived innumerable images, mainly of sadness. When, just four years old, he had attended his grandfather Mihalis' funeral and then when, ten years ago, he had been separated from Alison. Alison, who after her infrequent messages throughout their long separation, had now come back into his life to show that he was still in her mind and perhaps – why not? – in her heart. It took him a few minutes to concentrate: he decided to leave Alison's message an unsolved mystery and to read the other, the long message from his grandfather.

• • •

"I do not know who will read this message", began the elder Mihalis, "Whether it will be my son Yiorgos or someone else. However, I am writing this testimony in the hope that it will help at least a part of society to take the correct steps towards humanity and solidarity."

"Many years ago, I attended a seminar in America lasting several days. Its theme, "From Aristotle to Martin Luther King", looked at research into the fundamental ideas and human principles which have 'theoretically' dominated our history for two and half thousand years. The method used throughout the seminar was that of the Socratic Dialogue, in an effort to establish what, according to Aristotle, constituted happiness. Simultaneously, concepts such as morality, ethics, leadership, social justice, education and many others were discussed. I believe that many correct conclusions were arrived at, such as the fact that the existence of laws and a citizen's simple compliance does not replace the rightness of human relationships or the knowledge of goodness. Something more is needed since the above principles usually remain on the theoretical level and do not affect acts in everyday life. In reality, there is no political system which cannot develop into a dictatorship, particularly into a certain kind of economic tyranny. Of special significance in relation to

this is the 'greed' of powerful financial groups, belonging to those 'limitless' or rather 'savage' human desires which can never be effectively cured but demand serious effort on Society's part to contain them, if not completely eradicate them. Here I quote Plato in the 'Republic': 'There is in every one of us, even those who seem to be most moderate, a type of desire that is terrible, wild, and lawless.' In today's world, this characteristic is called, as we have already said, 'greed' and it is this which belongs to those 'wild desires' that cannot be cured but require continuous attention and special education. This wild desire has, as was stressed in the seminar, strange side effects. One of these was described by a Polish writer, a few years ago under exactly the same title, 'Greed'. In this book – a novel - he says that everywhere people, predicting general catastrophe and expecting some sort of hostile attack, run to find and take a pill that calms and instills a feeling of happiness. They do not take this pill because they have to but because their desire for peace and harmony goes deeper than their fear and desire to avoid physical catastrophe. And, according to reviewers of the book, this compulsion is nothing other than an image of people who, swallowing a pill in search of pleasure in their world, fail to realize that in the end it is the world that is swallowing them.

The seminar also concluded that there is a need to find ways of helping the principles and values that have been passed down to us by the great philosophers to become rooted in the thinking and will of leaders. In this way, leaders will not only lead by example but will also legitimize any sanction in cases of contrary behaviour. This unequivocally means that a revolution is needed in our system for electing leaders and shaping and educating them in the way they think and behave; in the need to maintain, as their priority, the feelings and needs of their people. For these reasons, society's greatest task is to provide its leaders with compulsory correct knowledge and correct education. The consequences, otherwise, particularly in a future where technology is ever-increasingly powerful, will be tragic. Because, as a certain philosopher of the twentieth century said:

"Man's capacity for justice makes Democracy feasible, but man's inclination to injustice renders Democracy necessary." (Reinhold Niebuhr (1892-1971)

Therefore our political life does not simply need a gentle change, it needs a revolution. There are two possible solutions to the leadership question: either to change the way we elect our leaders, something which is particularly difficult since a leader's background is often unknown or the arrogance of power changes his behavior; or to find a way of educating leaders after they have been elected so that they always keep actively in mind the thoughts and feelings of other citizens and are sincerely sensitive to their needs."

Michos felt confused by this admission of his Grandfather's. The elder Mihalis had been a scientist who specialized in computers at a time when this science was at its peak. The phrases used up to now reminded one more of a theoretician of political sciences. Michos pressed the key to continue his ancestor's description: *"I must stress that what follows constitutes the essence of my discovery and may be either a gift or a curse to the person I confide in. When I first announced it, people everywhere moved heaven and earth to get hold of it, to discover more about it, or even to hinder its implementation. It was considered so dangerous and subversive that its consequences for the future were judged by many to be cat astrophic. Catastrophic for human understanding and for our intellectual welfare. It concerns total control, through the tele-control of knowledge and thought. It was therefore considered a dangerous means since in the wrong hands it might lead to the enslavement of the human brain.*

To explain: Up to now, technology has been able to record data in the form of a unit, a "byte" as it is called whenever it is activated. I have proved, however, that there is another way: to concentrate data, thousands, millions, billions of "bytes" and to transmit them all at once. With one unique "electronic flash", not only from one computer to another, but from a computer to a human brain. Obviously, any such interference activates new experiences and knowledge in the brain and out of necessity pushes down into the depths of memory all that pre-dated it. It is thus a means that can be used for the group implantation of knowledge, both for well-intentioned purposes such as education as well as for dangerous activities such as total brainwashing by a dictatorial power.

I wrestled long and hard with mind and heart before I went ahead. I was hugely tormented by such thoughts and wondered whether I should pass

30

on the knowledge gained from my research or destroy it for fear it might be used by my successors in a way catastrophic for humanity. I hesitated until a year ago. However, society has been through so much over recent decades. First, it experienced those things for which international capital bore the main responsibility. With the shifting of the global economy from West to East, European leaders succeeded in destroying their peoples financially, with the result that three or four years ago the European Union broke up, despite the expectations for it of so many. Then there were the many religious con flicts, not only in Europe but throughout the world. The destructive wars over petrol in the Mediterranean and water in Asia also took place. I do not know what may further occur in the years to come, but all this has made me finally decide to confide my discovery in the manner I have done today, in the belief that my son or a descendent of mine will not only want to but will be able to make the correct, ethical use of this discovery. For this reason, I am handing over the technical details and information needed to define the method of application of this discovery which I have named, perhaps some-what hastily, "Accumulative-Monographic Tele-education".

Whatever is decided should be done with these means, with the knowl-edge that I am handing over, it is my wish that it have the best possible success for society in general and for each and every citizen in particular."
Mihalis D.

• • •

Michos had been sitting in this almost medieval vehicle for an hour and a half. He had decided to make the trip from Bishkek to Ak-Terek like one of the locals. Not only because an ancient bus was the least mon-itored means of transport but also to give him more time to think. To think about all the new details that had literally enveloped him over the last two days: the knowledge of his grandfather's secret, anxiety over his surveillance by the System – something confirmed by Alison's dis-creet message, his need to find help and the uncertainty concerning decisions already taken. As soon as he had read his grandfather's message, he understood that if he wanted to take some sort of action he would have to seek specialist help. Alternatively, the only other solution would be to dispose of the elder Mihalis' file to prevent it falling into the hands of people who would exploit the power it represented for their own gain. Because Michos was in no doubt that this secret contained all that was necessary to give immense power to whoever might use it, and particularly to whoever might use it for selfish purposes. He understood, however, that to give this secret the power he wished for it, he would need the help of two specialists: one with an advanced knowledge of the technology for the programming of modern computers and another, more difficult to find, with a wide knowledge of philosophy and a practical knowledge of the classical writers and the politics and cultural history of democratic institutions. He put these keywords into his "Logic" card, combined with the requirement that the individuals should be within a reasonable distance of Bishkek. He had very little time if his thoughts of finding any sort of application were to be translated into direct action.

His search produced two specific results. For the programming specialist, the "Logic" card gave him the name of a young man originally from Bangalore in India, the famous city where, over the past decades, computer businesses, research, engineering and telecommunications had developed. At the moment, the young man was working in a relatively nearby village, Ak-Terek, where the old bus was now taking him. Michos was impressed that, despite being exceptionally gifted according to the official information, the Indian was only 16 years old. His name was Babar Sarma and he was ranked 25th in programmer world ratings. Because it was known that the close surveillance of everyone by the Triptych System left no margin for error, Michos felt he could trust the information concerning the young man's level of competence. The second person to show up on the "Logic" card was a teacher. His location, according to the "Logic" card, was fairly close to Babar Sarma's village, but a strange place to say the least. It was level "A" "Purification" camp number 425. He was of Egyptian origin, his name Kamel Aizentin.

The bus journey had a relaxing effect on Michos. The decisions he had to take were not easy. Despite this, the route through the mountains, ending on the banks of Lake Issyk Koul shortly before sunset, had lifted his spirits and psyche. As if his thoughts had suddenly given wings to the idea that perhaps he really would do something beneficial for his fellow human beings. He smiled inwardly at the realization that unrelated objects and images were able to influence one's inner world in a variety of ways. He wondered whether he would have thought of the wings had there not been two Kyrgyz eagle hunters on the bus with him. These were relics of a community that had managed to get through recent decades thanks to tourism and, more recently, the need to survive. Looking as the very first eagle hunters must have done, they sat in the front seats, wearing the traditional head-covering, their double-curved bows beside them and enormous caged eagles in the aisle, their wings crushed each time the bus encountered a pothole.

"That's where the 'wings' came from," thought Michos, "Perhaps because even with wings I remain tightly bound to the System, just like these eagles next to me. When they are released for hunting, their 'bosses' keep a tight hold on them too, via long and sturdy hair-ropes.

• • •

Night had fallen by the time Michos found Babar Sarma's small house on the banks of the lake. It was made of wood and stone and built on the corner of a makeshift pier that extended about twenty metres into the water. It looked more like a fisherman's hut than the headquarters of an electronic programmer. His knock at the door was answered by a pleasantly fresh sounding voice.

"Coming!" It had a characteristically Indian tone. The door was opened by a tall, young man with a long and thin but pleasantly smiling face. There were the beginnings of a moustache on his upper lip and, between that and his jet black hair, Michos' attention was held by a fine, broad forehead and two highly intelligent dark eyes.

"I'm Michos, I sent you that message today." He said. "Welcome!" the youth replied. "Please enter my humble dwelling." His "humble dwelling" was far less than humble. It was a bedlam of papers, computers and clothes. Babar made room for him to sit on a bench between a stack of papers and a heap of dirty clothes. Before him on a small table were three computers variously dating from the early 21st century to the present, 2071. Babar made an apologetic gesture for the untidiness and asked his visitor what he would like to drink. Michos shook his head.

"I came as soon as I received your response to my message about the job as a representative with 'BIOP', the Bio-organic Pharmaceuticals Manufacturer. I was pleased with your positive response and I'm here so we can discuss the details." Michos had indeed sent this message, with a notification, to the headquarters of his multi-national company, because this allowed him to contact the programmer. He was sure that the same message had also been received by local heads of security and that this was the only reason why he had not as yet been paid a "visit" by the defenders.

"The whole world has heard of 'BIOP'", replied Babar who had sat down on a stool opposite Michos. "I'd be delighted to collaborate with them. It isn't that I haven't got work at present, but it does not allow me to continue my research...." He hesitated for a moment. "That is why I am here in such a remote place. It helps me concentrate..." He smiled.

At that moment the door to an adjoining room opened and a silhouette in a long, loosely-fitting, bright red dress appeared. "A Chinese woman", thought Michos, puzzled, but also anxious because her presence changed the scenario he had planned for his proposal to Babar.

"Your wife?" he asked politely. Babar laughed. "She is...... Yes, my companion". He was almost embarrassed by how old-fashioned his visitor seemed to be. Since when would a youth like himself have been married? "She is my very sweet Su. Her name is Su Dong and her country, China, has sent her to me as a consolation for my loneliness." He gestured her to approach. Su seemed to be the same age or perhaps a little older than Babar. She approached the visitor and greeted him with a slight bow of the head, her hands held together. Michos responded in the same manner. Su smiled and returned to the other room.

Michos weighed up the situation and decided to go ahead. In any case, there was no time left. His decision would lead either to the result he had planned or to the destruction of his grandfather's discovery. There was no time for hesitation.

He took a piece of paper from his pocket. On it was written something he had already prepared and, without saying a word, he pushed it across to Babar to read.

"I have another proposal to make to you, on condition that this remains a secret. Whatever we may wish to say about it must be written down and not spoken out loud. This is vital for your wellbeing as well as my safety."

Babar read it and his look became more animated. As if he had expected something like this. He turned towards the door from which his Chinese companion had appeared and called out, "Su, darling!"

For a moment Michos wanted to protest, to say that the aim was to keep the meeting as secret as possible, but he held back. Babar's expression indicated that he had been understood. Su came back into the room and Babar moved over so she could sit next to him.

"Our friend who has done us the honour of offering us a job in one of the biggest multinational companies on the planet would, I believe, like to hear your story," he said. "Please tell how you decided to come to India from your homeland and what role you play in the work we do together. Meanwhile I will serve our visitor a drink."

"What is your proposal?" he wrote hurriedly on the paper and showed it to Michos.

Michos had already prepared his reply on the reverse side of the paper.

"I am in possession of an important discovery. A discovery that can change the world as we know it, into the world that we want. There are risks that we will have to take. I want to know if you are prepared to take them with me. Your specialization and your expertise are absolutely essential for our success. And another thing: We have very little time."

"I am the great granddaughter of one of the students who became victims in Tiananmen Square in the last century." The room was still as Su began the narration of her life, as Babar had asked her. "My grandparents and parents had a very restricted life, despite the fact that positive developments resulting from that tragic event led to an improvement in their prospects - at least in the economic sense. So I got the opportunity to go to University, without however making much progress. At the same time I was working in the electronics in-dustry and I learned a lot...."

"The explanations must wait until tomorrow morning," wrote Babar on Michos' paper. "In the meantime, we will listen to Su. Put the card I will give you over your 'Logic' card, please." The young man got up and opened a drawer under the table. He took out a white luminous card similar in size to a "Logic" card and gave it to Michos. Understanding that Babar had good reason for this strange request, he placed the white luminous card over the "Logic" card in his pocket without asking for an explanation.

"I learned a lot in the industry," Su continued. "I also learned how to protect myself against everyday difficulties. Such as being stalked by men when I reached puberty. You know, with the one-child policy in China for so many decades, the number of women dramatically de-clined in comparison with men. They sought out women like maniacs, even ugly ones, she smiled. Don't ask me how that shortage of women came about. It was an act of inhumanity practiced by many farmers to ensure they had male descendants to help them with their heavy work. Thus I found myself obliged to accept a husband who I didn't like at all. He pushed me into accepting him by paying the dowry up-front, before the wedding. For many years now, you see, the practice has been for the fiancé to give a dowry to his intended bride, precisely because brides are so hard to come by. In the meantime, in the city where I worked, radioctivity was spreading from the South China nuclear explosion some years earlier. An explosion for which no one was ever held responsible but which wiped out many millions of people. So, two days before the wedding I made a big decision. I took the dowry and a few clothes and crossed over the western border. I found myself in Bangalore and there I met Babar..." She laughed and gave him an adoring look.

"I think it's time we left our guest to get some rest," Babar interrupted her. "You'll have time to continue your story tomorrow." Turning to Michos, "I'll prepare your bed," he said. "Tomorrow morning we'll talk more about the representative's job you've offered me and you'll hear the rest of Su's story".

3
CRIMSONDAY

A pleasant, almost childlike smile confronted Michos when he woke up on the morning of the Third day. He had slept deeply without being disturbed by the twittering of the birds on the lake. The smile was Babar's and in his hands he was holding a hot cup of tea and a pirozhki for breakfast.

"I slept well," Michos said as he drank his tea. He nodded to show his pleasure.

"Better than you think," replied Babar still smiling. Michos looked at him without understanding what the young man meant. He began to eat his pirozhki. "Does Su cook?" he asked. "When necessary, yes, but we share those jobs just like all the others. May I have your 'Logic' card?" Babar said unexpectedly.

Puzzled, Michos looked at him but immediately took the card out of his bag, with the luminous card Babar had given him the previous evening. The young man put the cards together and pressed on certain parts of them. He nodded. He was satisfied.

Michos watched in silence, awaiting an explanation. After all, Babar was the expert. Or at least that is what he hoped.

"We can now speak and say whatever we need to without any danger," said Babar finally. "I'll explain. Some time ago, together with colleagues in India, we found a way to bypass the process that keeps us constricted by the 'Logic' card. The antidote has been found, I would say. I personally have named it 'Para-logic'. It is this luminous card that I gave you yesterday." He held it up. "This temporarily cancels many functions of the official card, but it also saves them and reproduces them whenever it is asked to do so. For example, to put it simply: yesterday evening I ordered the 'Para-logic' card to reproduce the hours of your sleep, and now I've put it into operation to activate those hours. This reproduction passes from the white, luminous card into your 'Logic' card for any interested party who is watching you at this moment. The result: We are able to speak freely for a few hours, that is, exactly for the length of time you were asleep."

Babar could not avoid a smile of triumph, a little like a mischievous child who has just managed to do something outrageous. "Et voila!" he added.

Michos was speechless. His expression must have shown admiration because Babar's smile became even broader.

"So, now I can speak and I don't have to write it down..."

"Exactly! Whatever we say will remain between ourselves," the young man assured him.

"When did you discover this?" Michos wanted to know. "An old tradition gave us the idea," Babar was thoroughly enjoying this. He paused. "From guerrilla fighters in Sierra Leone. They used to say that they had an 'invisible witch' on their side. A witch who went ahead of them into battle. She would be naked and walking backwards holding a mirror turned towards the enemy. This, they believed made her invisible and able to get behind the opposing army where she could perform her magic to increase the chances of victory for her side. Our 'Para-logic' card plays the same role. It makes us invisible and allows us to defend ourselves against the continuous surveillance of the Triptych System." Michos smiled and, without hiding his satisfaction, told the story of his grandfather's discovery. He ended with the thoughts he had had the previous day: "My problem is," he said, "That this whole programme of my grandfather's has to be updated to make it compatible with today's computers so that I can pass on certain knowledge - I will explain the details to you later - to the central information transmitter, implanted by the System, through electronic hypnosis. I believe that many positive things can be brought about through such an intervention..."

"Intervention or revolution?"

"They can call it what they like. As long as it is positive for mankind..."

Babar seemed skeptical.

"Does what I said frighten you?"

"I can't pretend otherwise. It does frighten me. But it's not only that. There is another obstacle to the....intervention as you call it."

"What is it? You understand that we have to clarify a lot of things before we start and there isn't much time. They may not know what we are up to at the central surveillance system, but just the fact that I haven't stuck to my fixed schedule will have been noted and it won't be long before the Defenders get here."

"To achieve any result, the messages or knowledge, as you said, have to reach the upper echelons of power. But there we have a problem. Those echelons use the gold 'Logic' cards and not the bronze or silver ones like ours. What I can do with our cards is not going to have any effect on top members of the leadership unless I have a gold card in my hands. And I've never even seen a gold card."

Michos felt as if he had been drenched in cold water, after the satisfaction he had felt at the beginning of his discussion with the young man. He racked his brains trying to find a solution.

The solution was to find a gold card nearby and put it in Babar's hands, for him, if possible, to produce the appropriate result.

"How many hours can I continue being invisible and silent on my 'Logic' card?" he asked finally.

. . .

At an altitude of over two thousand metres, Michos just had time to make out the sign for "Karakol" as the air-car slowed down. In a brief history of the area, Babar had explained to him that it used to be a big tourist centre until the lake became contaminated by repeated spillage from a gold mine operating in the area. The accidents had begun in the twentieth century. The first was when a large tanker carrying acids for the mine had plunged down the mountainside into the lake. Then, the head of the region, to demonstrate to the tourists that the lake was safe for swimming, ordered the local ecology official to make a public show of personally swimming in the lake. It was never known what became of the official, or whether the head had been prepared to make the same sacrifice for the benefit of local tourism. There were also other causes of contamination and tourism in the area collapsed. Since Karakol was now unable to accommodate tourists, it was selected to become one of the first Purification Camps. This was where an anxious Kamel had arrived a few hours earlier to find his wife and children. Babar's final piece of information was exactly where Michos would need to go to find Kamel. This was an old, wooden religious monument used by the camp administration as a coordination centre.

The air-car stopped in the central square of the once touristic town and Michos walked from there until he found the "religious monument" described by Babar. Made of the wood from trees in the local forest, it was simply an old church which looked about to collapse. The idea of asking for an Egyptian he did not know and who had perhaps been accused of some sort of crime against the System did not thrill Michos. On the other hand, he knew that to find the only person indicated by the System's Information Centre as being in the vicinity and having the knowledge and experience needed to carry out his plan, he would have to ask, even if it were dangerous. Inwardly, he felt resigned. The rest of his life was now predictable. It would be permanently accompanied by danger. With no let-ups.

He went up to the entrance of the old church and asked the first employee sitting behind a desk where he could find Kamel Aizentin. The young man was very polite. He took a form from a nearby stack of papers, gave it to Michos and asked him to fill it in. Michos went over to a table not far from the young man. The questions on the form were simple: name and profession of applicant as well as of the person with whom he was requesting a meeting, purpose of the meeting and his signature.

The first details were not a problem for Michos to complete. He hesitated a little over the reason for the meeting. However, he found a sort of solution which, if not absolutely sincere at first sight, with a little imagination might be found credible. He wrote down that his work was to promote the great "Bio-Organic Pharmaceuticals Company" (BIOP) and the purpose of the meeting was to secure the services of a scientist capable of helping him with the advertising of what he described as "people friendly" pharmaceuticals. This person had to have a broad knowledge of philosophy and a practical knowledge of classical writers, cultural history and humanitarian institutions. "The Central System has informed me that Kamel Aïzentin has this knowledge." Michos added.

• • •

The four pointed domes of the wooden church finally appeared as Kamel left the last mountain top behind him before approaching the plateau of the old town. They had informed him that he was urgently wanted in the centre of Karakol and he had left the camp immediately. Not only because he had no choice but because it was such a bizarre demand. No one ever risked asking to meet a person already in the camp. Any connection with such a person could lead to serious consequences from the System. It did not forgive such relationships and moreover did everything to prevent any contact between those inside and those outside the camp. "And especially in this case," thought Kamel, having learned about what the future held for those inside.

He took the road leading down into the centre of the town, increasingly curious to see who was asking for him. He was afraid to make any supposition or prediction. And he was right. When he asked at the church entrance, they pointed out a total stranger. He had a pleasant and earnest face was tall and in his forties with grey eyes that reflected uncommon strength and will. The stranger came forward and put out his hand. He introduced himself and Kamel responded with his own name.

"Did you put in a request to see me?" he asked. Michos nodded. "It's about a collaboration that I would like to propose to you," he said. "It would be better though for us to sit down. Those benches in the courtyard will be more comfortable, I think."

The summer weather was misleading. The sun shone brightly but the wind blowing down from the surrounding mountains, rising to three thousand metres with their summits still snow-covered, was barely tolerable. Kamel wrapped his overcoat tightly around himself and sat down beside his unexpected visitor.

Making it up as he went along, Michos began to explain his reasons for requesting the meeting as described on the visitors' form and the needs of the advertising campaign for his pharmaceuticals. Something that was not too difficult since this was all part of his work. While he spoke, he took two sheets of paper from his pocket and passed them discreetly to Kamel.

"This will give you more details about the requirements of the job." The main points of grandfather Mihalis' discovery were written there. "And here you will see information about our next meeting, if of course you agree." The second paper was folded in two. In the fold was the luminous card borrowed from Babar and a brief text gave Kamel instructions on how to use it so that they might talk for a few hours without fear of being overheard.

44

The flood of information from the stranger had left Kamel speechless. A quick glance at the first page alarmed him. His response was definitely negative, or rather it would have been negative, if this meeting and the proposal for a collaboration had taken place the previous day. His intention and the purpose of his presence in this strange and inhospitable Asian village were simple: to do whatever he could to free his wife and children. And if he was unable to achieve this, he had thought of staying with them until the System decided that his family had reformed and was ready, with him, to be reinstated into free society. However, the terrible news that had leaked out at the camp did not allow him to refuse the proposal before having thought about it carefully, soberly assessing all the angles and the amount of danger posed by a positive response on the one side and a negative response on the other; a response that he had to give to this man with the grey eyes sitting beside him, and waiting for his answer. "In fact," he thought, "How do I know that he isn't an informer and isn't going to involve me in some crude provocation of the System? Or that, more simply, he isn't just insane?"

He looked Michos in the eye. His steady gaze with a faint suggestion of anxiety lessened Kamel's doubts.

"My first thought is the welfare of my family," Kamel felt he had to say. "That's my primary concern and looking for a job is a very secondary consideration right now."

"I completely understand," replied Michos. "That is why I suggest we meet again tomorrow morning here, in the same place. That way, your answer will be based on clearer thought following a good night's sleep..." he added, discreetly indicating the small sheet of paper with the luminous card that Kamel was still holding.

4
BLUSHDAY

"Everything began with the great financial crisis. But was that really true?" Kamel wondered, as for the second time in twenty four hours he made the journey down from the camp to the wooden church of Karakol. No, it had not happened like that. The crisis was not the cause but the result of a much more serious and more general crisis. A crisis of ethical values and of the basic principles of humanitarianism and solidarity. A crisis stemming from contempt for the truth and the balances that must exist in a society of people who feel that their life is worth living. A civilization collapses, not because its philosophical basis relating to the world changes, but because the ambitions, the dogmatism, the greed and corruption of those – people and organizations – who make up the administrative structures have distanced themselves from or forgotten those foundations.

The camp he had just left was the proof. Each inmate there had not only abandoned all thought of supporting his fellow inmates but also any hope of self-preservation and any defensive suggestion that might demonstrate the slightest sign of self-esteem. In other words, abandonment; and this perhaps explained the near in-difference with which the appalling information that had just begun to circulate was received.

The story had started some decades earlier. "It is my wish that we will be ready to send the first man to Mars within 10 to 15 years," some billionaire founder of a giant company had said during an interview on the BBC. Many more than the predicted 10 – 15 years went by. Indeed, at some point he had stated:

"We can't wait all that much longer because I don't want to be too old to go." And his last act had been to place an order for a spaceship named Dragon, intended for the transportation of personnel and cargo to the International Space Station. This same daring businessman was never lucky enough to take his dream journey. He had died many years ago. Now, however, the Triptych System had approved a programme named "Persephone" in Ancient Greek mode. It was soon to send a large number of people in a "space arc" to the same, "silent" planet as had been envisaged by the American businessman. The System had decided that it should select individuals who were not only physically and mentally strong, but who could also serve as guinea pigs, disposable human beings. It was therefore natural for selection to turn to the colonies in the Purification Camps, to man at least the first experimental missions.

"And yet," thought Kamel again, as he descended the road on the last phase of the journey, "I can't say I'd be able to decide if I could only choose between being held in a camp for the rest of my life or taking a one-way ticket into space."

The great problem with the first option is not just the synthetic food you are given. Genetically modified food belongs to the past; it is thought of as the only natural form of food and has become very rare. What is handed out in the Purification Camps was a wholly synthetic mixture of organic and inorganic substances. It is not the tight control exercised over an inmate while in a camp either; nor is it the investigation of each inmate's background, all the way back to one's great-grandfather. It is not even the absence of any hope of ever restarting one's former life of freedom. No, the most tragic aspect is the constant striving of parents to stay alive for as long as possible, so that their children are not left parentless. Because then they are certain to be transferred to the special camp section for "unaccompanied children", from where, it was widely rumoured, they would very soon disappear. Organ transplants for organizations of ageing, First Caste citizens had become so common that it would be odd if they did not use the organs of those healthy young people who in any case had not long to live. "The philosophy of Kaiada in reverse," thought Kamel as he spotted Michos sitting patiently on the bench outside the wooden church.

"How's the family?" Michos began the conversation while making a sign to Kamel about the whereabouts of his "Para-logic" card".

"Alright, for the moment." Kamel showed him the two cards pressed together.

"We can speak freely now," said Michos. "Have you thought about my proposal? I mean the one on the piece of paper?"

"It's not difficult for me to give you the data you want," replied Kamel. "And if there are things I can't remember off by heart, I can look them up."

"How quickly?" Michos pressed him. "Maybe even by tomorrow". "Could you give them to somebody who will be coming to find you tomorrow? It'll be the man who will transfer them into the system they are intended for..."

"I could. But I'm wondering if the end result is worth the danger involved."

"Dangers exist, I don't deny it. This act of mine was described by the friend I just mentioned as a revolution. But don't forget what Machiavelli said. That disobedience, in the eyes of whoever has read history, is the first virtue of mankind. Disobedience has given birth to progress – progress stemming from disobedience and revolution. But this will be a new kind of revolution. Once revolutions took place through the masses, but today they would be doomed to failure. The System's control has been so perfected that there is no doubt about that. Today, in the way that I'm proposing, I believe revolution can be carried out by as few people as can be counted on the fingers of one hand. Without victims. Without upheavals. Without supporters."

"Except for us, of course," said Kamel.

"Except for us," agreed Michos. "Do you still have any doubts? I need to know."

"For me, the fate of my family is my first concern. My own fate is completely secondary. Because I see no hope for the first, I'm indifferent to the second. That's why I'm with you, and perhaps we'll succeed."

"The experts believe it. If you give them enough data to download." Michos took a small packet of mnemonema from his pocket and passed them to Kamel. Mnemonema had replaced "memory sticks" for storing data decades ago. These, apart from their compatibility with the "Logic" card, were capable of storing data many times greater in quantity than the once familiar memory stick.

"You will have it tomorrow," replied Kamel as he put the mnemonema packet inside his jacket "If it is true that the all-mighty of information technology has given us knowledge irrelevant to peoples' pursuit of happiness, or if what a famous writer, Oscar Wilde, said is true that people have descended to the level of having an insatiable curiosity for knowing everything except for what is worth becoming known - if that is true, then something may change with the discovery of your ancestor. You will have all the knowledge and wisdom of the ancient and modern humanists and philosophers. Every call for mankind to morally rectify itself. Every action noted for the constructive progress it brought about. There will be expansions on Plato's "All the gold which is under or upon the earth is not enough to give in exchange for virtue"; everything up to and including John Naisbitt, who predicted that "The most exciting breakthroughs of the 21st century will not occur because of technology but because of an expanding concept of what it means to be human."

• • •

"I keep telling you that I want to see the world, the other world."
Klara had not stopped complaining to Amsey all morning about feeling
bored. She had got into her head the idea that, come what may, she
had to get to the Asian coastline opposite and see for herself how "the
others" lived. Amsey had tried to convince her that such an act would
be very dangerous because, particularly along that coastline, there was
no organized presence of defenders and her protectors would be furious if Amsey allowed her to leave her floating palace. In any case, she
reminded Klara, one of her protectors was to join her the next day.
Klara however was adamant and put forward another argument.
Searching through information on the area where the luxury craft was
moored, she had found an interesting new piece of information that
had particularly aroused her curiosity. A short distance from where
they were there was an ancient historical monument, an entire ancient
city, the city of Troy. "Where the Trojan war was fought," she declared,
pleased with the knowledge she had just acquired.

"There is nothing of importance for you to see", said Amsey in
an attempt to reject the idea. "Only ruins, and those are reconstruc-
tions. And a 'Trojan Horse', falling to bits, constructed at the turn of
the century for visitors to take photographs of each other posing in
the windows opened along its flanks. Nothing of significance, I'm telling you. But most importantly, that good gentleman Hassan Porter
who is visiting you tomorrow will be furious if he finds out – and he
will of course find out – that you have been out on the Asian coast
just before his arrival."

"I'm telling you that I want to see. See for myself what 'the others'
do. Outside, in their own world. When the System was set up, I was
only five years old and I don't remember anything. Since then, I've
been living in a golden cage and it's starting to suffocate me. I sometimes think that perhaps someone could help, that is, if some of those
people need help."

"You live a life of pleasure which very few have. Believe me, you
are among the very fortunate of this world. And I'll tell you something

else: you are lucky not to know what sort of life 'the others' - as you put it - live. Because it is so different from yours that you would despair if you were to see it with your own eyes. Because you have a good heart, my dear Klara, and you will see that you cannot help those 'others', in any way. You are not only unable to help them, you are not allowed to. It is one of the rules that cannot be broken."

She went up to Klara and embraced her. "You know that I want what is best for you," she murmured. "Help, such as it is, for those in the 'other' world is undertaken by the System. Each act of help that happens to be offered directly by citizens of our category will be considered seditious. Like those that took place in past decades, before the establishment of the System. Personal initiatives are not permitted and the institutions are no longer adequate to change life 'outside'. People's souls have to change. Only then will they feel free again. But it is impossible for that to happen....."

• • •

Amsey could not believe her eyes. The message on the card was from Michos. It was not like others that she had exchanged with him from time to time: stereotyped, friendly and distant. He was asking her where he could meet her, and as soon as possible. She could not weigh up the consequences that such a move might have for Michos. She was certain these would be serious because he would be breaking a condition that had been imposed on him almost ten years ago: never to meet her again or even ask for such a thing. For her, moreover, the consequences were sure to be catastrophic. She had been nominated for membership of the group that had for months now been organiz ing the Great Celebration to honour the tenth anniversary of the foundation of the Triptych System. The work she was doing for this significant event was certain to secure her a better future. At least, she hoped so. Now, however, if she agreed to meet Michos, everything would be ruined. There would be no hope of continuing the life she had led up to now. No hope of remaining free. No hope, perhaps, of even seeing the sun again tomorrow.

She leant against the handrail. But the beauty of the island before her could not hold her attention. The gently rolling sea which she usually loved to watch only increased her nausea. Nausea brought on by fear. To say "No" was the only logical thing to do. The restrictions imposed on them allowed for no other solution. It was the only way to avoid ruination for both of them. Michos had to understand that. But this message was different from those she had come to know from the man she had once loved. It had something.....she would have said, beyond them both as individuals. Beyond any wish, the future, chance or material concern on a personal level. Beyond the very existence of two people who had loved each other so strongly and who, she believed, still loved each other.

Something else made today's message from Michos different. Like the previous one, it contained something that touched her. The language he used. It was written in the language she had taught him when they had been together. To amuse themselves, she had decided to teach him the strange and largely forgotten language of the Navajo, passed down to her by her father. Within the family, they had kept up a tradition started during the Second World War in the mid-twentieth century. One of her ancestors had helped create a code based on the language of the tribe; this code had never been cracked by the enemy, the Japanese, despite all their efforts. Amsey, at that time Alison, had enjoyed teaching Michos this code. She never imagined then that now, so many years later, he would remember it and even send her a message that day using it.

• • •

The conviction he brought to his every action was – and he was proud of this – the main characteristic of the way he performed his duties. On this Wednesday, however, Kasper had stumbled on an inexplicable detail while preparing his daily report. He hesitated briefly and then ordered his portable computer to return to the beginning of the text. The computer he wore was a light-weight helmet, very similar to the old headsets worn by pop groups, and it received instructions from the wearer's thoughts, a technological breakthrough following experimentation back in the mid-century. This technology was not available to just anyone however, but only to high ranking officials. And as a Triptych System controller for Eastern Europe and the Middle East region, Kasper was one of them.

The computer first showed a picture of Kasper himself, on the large screen opposite. He had programmed it so that, with every new task, he would have the pleasure of seeing his own face, something which increased his confidence to perform the day's work. It was the eyes that dominated the face he was looking at now; light green in colour, intelligent, with vitality to spare and attractive, despite the fact that behind the strong appearance a certain tell-tale cruelty was discernible. Above the eyes, two fine and perfectly straight eyebrows gave the required masculinity to his face that was of light complexion with a straight, aristocratic nose and full lips. These were usually slightly parted, as if about to recite a poem. Completing the picture, his face was framed by long side-burns and a fine, light-coloured beard.

After his picture, the text that appeared on the screen was both concise and comprehensive, like all his reports to the TCI - the Tripartite Committee of Inspectors.

"I hereby report three contraventions and how they were dealt with:

a) The first relates to a certain citizen of Sana'a, in Yemen. In defiance of TS instructions, the person named Gamal Samir subjected his wife to inhumane punishment because she had conceived after six years of married life. Gamal, who had not fathered a child by any other woman, was convinced that he was sterile and suspected that his wife was pregnant as the result of an extra-marital affair. In the past, such a suspicion would have been reason enough for the woman to be put to death by stoning, but TS rules and recent reforms have outlawed such a practice and her treatment would be removal to a category B camp. However, as punishment, Gamal Samir bound his wife in chains and buried her alive in the desert with only a tube to breathe through. Naturally, as soon as I learned of the incident, I sent defenders to arrest him and hand him over to his homeland's Justice System. His wife survived as a result of this prompt action.

b) The second contravention relates to a Lebanese citizen Farid Bitar. When his father died two months ago, he received the relevant P.C. (property credit) documents for the deceased and misappropriated them, ignoring the TS rule which states that heirs are only entitled to an inheritance – as it was once called – of ten per cent of the deceased's fortune. Naturally, in this case I sent defenders who applied the law by returning the misappropriated amount of P.C. to the Payments Department of the TS, and handing him over to the Courts.

c) The third contravention relates to a travelling salesman for a large pharmaceuticals company in the Middle East. His movements seemed at best strange to me when he was in Bishkek for professional reasons. A certain delay in his schedule first attracted computer attention and then the individual named Michos Diakakis travelled from Bishkek to Lake Issyk Koul. His movements suggest the involvement of others and I am following developments to ascertain what activities they are planning and who these other people are. With regard to this, I defer my full report until such time as these matters become clearer.

Signed, Kasper Controller, Eastern Europe and the Middle East"

Kasper turned this over in his mind for a few moments, gauging the conclusion that an Inspector reading the report might arrive at, and decided that it was satisfactory for the System's operation as well as for his personal image. He took one more look at his own face on the screen and his eyes narrowed with pleasure. He was not just anybody, he thought. His origins went back to the beginning of the century when eugenics was still in its infancy and objections outweighed scientific support. The objections were throwbacks explained by memories of Nazi activity, when various inhumane and racist experiments were carried in an attempt to strengthen their "Aryan Race".

There had however been a revival of such research during the first decades of the 21st century, with primitive interventions then referred to as positive and negative eugenics. At first, the purpose had been to prevent health problems through a method for relieving people of those imperfect genes responsible for specific diseases. This method had moved, imperceptibly, mainly in northern Europe, into another, closer to that of the Nazis and less relevant to scientific investigation. Beyond, that is, cures for diseases, there was a search for improvement of the human as a species: the creation of "genotypic" and "phenotypic" human characteristics, equivalent to the improvement of the "internal world" and external appearance of the species. The main method for the introduction of these characteristics consisted of the implantation of viruses, enriched with the appropriate characteristics taken by scientists from embryos cultivated "in vitro", popularly referred to as "test-tubes". Kasper's "production" began in 2020, under excellent conditions and with original characteristics eminently suitable for the creation of an individual with particularly well developed intellectual abilities, as well as a pleasingly improved external appearance. He, together with another couple of dozen similar creations of science, constituted the perfect workers, loyal, respectable and effective organs of the System. Of the System which, when it had assumed its official form ten years ago, had, at the ready, these appropriate tools for its own seamless and unopposed promotion.

"I am the perfect worker for the System; without weaknesses, doubts or foolish pangs of conscience, working to counter every instance of contravention of the System's rules," thought Kasper with self-perception. A self-perception over which, nonetheless, a shadow had been cast by the difficulty he now faced in understanding a second message sent by the third transgressor, Michos Diakakis. There had been a first message in which the transgressor communicated with some systemic "companion" in the Aegean. However, the second message that had just arrived had completely baffled him. All his computer's efforts to interpret this second message had failed. He realized that his inability to deal with this matter like the other two, as well as innumerable others in the past, was due precisely to this message. He could not end his report by admitting that he had received a message that he himself could not understand, because the message was written in an incomprehensible language. Such a report would be unacceptable.

• • •

Amsey could not believe her eyes as she read Michos' second message. She wondered if he had gone completely mad. One of them must be deluded. It was impossible that he should be asking her to do what she was now reading in the wonderful code of her tribe.

"Dear Alison," it began, "I find myself forced to take a road with no return. Only you might be able to help. I must find a gold 'Logic' card to use for a few hours. I will explain everything to you. Yours ever, Michos."

"He is mad. He must be mad," thought Amsey as she returned to Klara's room to prepare her for the next day's visitor. Hassan Porter was one of the most important figures in the global industry of news production and control of News Media; he also participated in the wider sphere of political power and undoubtedly influenced even the top leaders of the Triptych System. The money at his disposal was limitless and the people around him all had powerful contacts. It was essential for Klara's welfare that the visit give him complete satisfaction, and the one responsible for this outcome was not only Klara but the organizer of the visit, Amsey, as well.

Klara was doing some gentle exercise on a treadmill. Her face lit up when she saw Amsey.

"Where were you, I was looking for you," she cried, stopping off the machine - Klara never exerted herself much regarding exercise.

"I was on deck, getting a little air," Amsey replied.

"I've told you it does us good to get out from time to time." Klara's tone suggested a reminder of her recent plea for them to go ashore on the coast of Asia Minor.

"The air on deck is harmless."

"Do you believe that one should live without danger? Without even the slightest danger?"

"I believe that life is full of dangers, even today when everything is said to be so safe. Even for members of our caste who have everything pre-planned and pre-paid, whose food has gone through every refinement and countless controls, who are surrounded by defenders to protect them, who are not threatened by unidentified people at public events – they used to be called 'demonstrations'. Now, even the thought of taking to the streets to demonstrate is punished by the authorities - despite all that we have, we have not secured the total absence of danger and that's why we have to consider every move we make."

Once more running at a gentle pace, Klara continued to look Amsey right in the eye.

"And yet I would like to know what being locked up in here is protecting me from." She persisted. "What, let's say, is Hassan, who will come to make love to me tomorrow, protecting me from..."

Noticeably irritated, she stepped off the treadmill. "And what is such life worth, locked up waiting for the man who will fuck me, so that I may be rewarded with four identical, cloned dogs or a previously savage animal made technically docile, or even this floating villa for me to travel around on, and you, even you, making me sick by going on about how lucky I am to be living in this.... Okay, for once I'll say it - this glitzy prison?"

Klara's outburst is a sudden revelation for Amsey. Her first thought is to calm her down. She lays her hands on Klara's shoulders. "Believe me," she says gently, "The only thing I want is your happiness. That's the role I've been given, and it's a role that I've accepted because you're a good person, I respect you and I love you. I just don't want you to come to any harm. You don't deserve it, believe me."

Klara tosses back her head. It is obvious she has run out of patience.

"It's all words," she murmurs. "Words without meaning, without real life. Without what I want to learn and experience, before our aristocracy tires of me. Before they tire of me like they tired of you, as soon as you turned thirty and stopped pretending to be a little girl." She broke free of Amsey and angrily stormed out towards the staircase leading up to the deck. Alarmed, Amsey followed her. The last thing she wanted was Klara on deck in her present state of mind.

"Listen to me!" she said as she followed. "I'll find a way for you to learn about life 'outside'. I give you my word that I'll do it right now. But you won't be happier then. On the contrary. The misery out there is so great that for once you'll regret having learned about something". Klara stopped on the top step and turned to look at her. Amsey, seeing that her friend's anger was fading, led her to her own favourite spot for looking out to sea up to the deck, where they leaned on the handrail side by side.

"But before I let you go 'out'," she murmured to Klara, "I'll give you something to read that you will keep to yourself. It was sent to me in secret this summer when I was working on the preparations for the Triptych System's tenth anniversary celebrations. It is a banned piece of writing and you must keep it secret. I don't want you put in danger because of me. The System is deadly serious about such matters."

Amsey was able to speak without fear of being overheard because in the "floating villa" - as they called it - the rule about the distance a

"Logic" card holder could be from his or her card did not apply to the two women, who always left them in their handbags in their rooms.

"What does it say?" asked Klara. Her dislike of reading was common knowledge. She rarely read anything that was not about fashion, or mindless news about the ostentatious international celebrities who played some sort of role in high society.

"It's a piece of writing by someone who knows how to give an account not only of today's situation but about how and why, since the beginning of the century, our society has reached this point. Let's go down and I can give it to you."

Very soon Klara was absorbed in the piece of writing Amsey had given her.

FROM THE SEWER THE YEAR 2062 The end of the twentieth century was not ideal. There were, as always, the rich and the poor. The developed and stagnant economies. Democracies and dictatorships. Liberal economies and the state subsidy mentality. Private wealth and state wealth. Everything was characterized, to a greater or lesser extent, by inequality. These were tolerable conditions however; a sort of balance following decades of world wars and the struggles for workers' rights. And everything had found this balance because two political giants dominated the world. The so-called Socialist East and the Capitalist West. Society began to change with the collapse of the Socialist East and the preeminence of the Capitalist West. This change had an immediate impact: societies lost the power they had derived from the democratic system – a system previously necessary to distinguish the West of freedom from the East of oppression – and fell into the net of international capitalism. Democracies ceased to have the same reason for their existence as they had under the former situation, when they served to distinguish between the "good" and "bad" society. Elections were now a matter for the few to control, through the power of capital, and to decide indirectly – via representatives – for the many. Money, increasingly in fewer and fewer hands, was able to control the masses more and more. The next step was the organization of globalism. The movement of capital and merchandise between countries was completely deregulated leading to those in southern Europe being overcharged. Investments no longer benefitted those who had the money, since returns in the real economy did not bring as much profit as products on the stock market secured. When the organs of the European Union – as it was then – gave priority to the high-technology products of the northern countries leading to the decline of the agricultural products of the southern countries, whatever was left of the competitiveness of the latter was destroyed and led to their being overcharged. In addition to all this came the economic nationalism of the united Germany, which managed to impose its hegemony and negate the basic values – equality and solidarity between countries - supported by the original creators of the European Union. Capital and technology were transferred to where wages were lowest, that is, to Asia. Thus, capital increased tenfold, millionaires multiplied and the developed countries began to suffer endemic unemployment; the middle class was destroyed and the poor became poorer. The very poor began killing each other or migrating to countries where they believed there was more hope of not dying of hunger.

However, these conditions made manipulation of society by the powerful even more necessary, and for this reason the system of thought control, which until then had only operated at an elementary level, was perfected. The various methods in existence were unified and controllers of mass media were trained in the use of new methods to make them as efficient as possible. Companies were set up which devised focused and convincing messaging, to encourage the passivity of citizens. Every political solution had to be presented as a choice taken by the citizens themselves, regardless of how completely it had been imposed by those in power, without citizens being aware of the consequences for themselves. Not only was education orientated towards these undertakings, but young people's extracurricular activities also had to fulfill a special agenda. This was directed at restricting any sort of reaction or even simple action from youngsters to confrontation with non-existent beasts, monsters and dragons; in other words, mythological or newly created enemies, beings belonging to another world and not existing in reality. In this way, technology for orienting young people's brains enables them to be kept in a state of vigilance against non-existent dangers and in a state of hypnosis regarding existing ones; in other words, the dangers of spiritual de-sensitizing and complete enslavement.

Furthermore, widespread use of the Internet by young people over pre-vious decades gave the ruling powers opportunities not only to focus the thoughts of future citizens on non-existent dangers, but also, with the aid of technology, to develop a system for directly influencing their brains. The many experiments began with an effort to treat traumatized ex-soldiers from third world combat zones, using methods for freeing them from their traumas. But these experiments also produced unwanted results such as suicides and other negative consequences. These included mind control and the obliteration of human sentiment, free thinking and moral scruples. Excessive use of infor-mation from the Internet, instead of producing more security of personal data, results in greater opportunities for the ruling powers to delve into the details of a person's everyday life, on the pretext of safe-guarding his security.

Thus, a few decades after the phenomenon of globalization, formerly developed societies ceased to be developed. After the huge increase in unem-ployment came the impoverishment of the middle and lower social classes, the break-up of the economic middle class in the West and the fragmentation of its society. To this were added serious internal imbalances in the developing countries. The collapse of European competitiveness created the need for re-ductions in wages in the then European Union, the invitation for immigrants to become cheap labour and, finally, recession, crisis and impoverishment. Characteristically, while in the past Europeans had seemed to be moving "to-wards an ever more united Europe", following the catastrophes left by this crisis, voters were repulsed at the mere mention of the creation of a United States of Europe. So, not only was competitiveness lost during the third decade of the century, but the European Union broke up completely. Social unrest followed: religious clashes, massacres, revolutions and wars over petrol and water. Via computer games featuring war techniques, the younger generation had received appropriate training. An obvious example was the enormous advertising campaign to launch the game "Call of Duty: Modern Warfare". This "game", through brilliant programming, reflected exactly what the fu-ture held.

Apart from the contrived "battle" scenarios created by the empire of television spectacle, it changed the manner of presenting real conflict in warfare. This was no longer presented following a time lapse but in productions with real battles in live transmissions showing the total destruction of entire villages and towns, and with people being blown to pieces at a distance determined only by how far the viewer was from his screen. In this way, wars were profitable for the TV channels owners, but also had an interim effect: young people in the US and the West were thus prepared and programmed to be obedient soldiers and cannon fodder since, when ordered, they willingly went out on the streets to fight 'maniacal terrorists and foreigners'. From the ashes of those conflicts emerged a new society, whose source of power was the Triptych System.

However, the situation in both East and West deteriorated socially through the deep gulf between the people and their leaders. This led to a serious crisis of the former's trust in governments and the financial system. Finally, conditions reached the point of dividing society and creating a universal sense of insecurity. Two years earlier, this led to an unprecedented repression of freedoms and workers' rights, coinciding with the Triptych System's consolidation of power and, in essence, the negation of every democratic idea and principle. The need for cheap labour, even in the primary sector, brought changes in established conditions such as the number of working hours, working days and months in the year. The working day was increased to twelve hours, the names of the days of the week were changed so that any association with specific religions (Sunday for Christians, Saturday for Jews, Friday for Muslims) was lost, and the number of days in a week increased to eleven (ten working days and one rest day); the year now had eleven months. With regard to payment for labour, various methods were used by those in control to force it down to the levels of Asia. One of these was the provocation of internal conflicts in the East aimed at creating a great flow of refugees to the West, in order to secure a cheap workforce for Europe.

Many years ago, there had been a public outcry when the prime minister of a South American country decided to make child labour legal from the age of twelve. He maintained that this decision was necessary since family incomes were dependent upon child labour, even if the children were very young. Although this phenomenon had been an exception at the time, with the global imposition of the Triptych System it has now become the norm, the lower age limit being fixed at between twelve and fourteen: local authorities judge it is necessary for them to base the survival of the economy on child labour. Since nothing comes cheaper. Not even refugees.

All this triggered tragic events in Europe and the rest of the world. Inhuman religious conflicts, massacres and destruction became everyday occurrences. It seemed impossible for the situation to resolve itself using the existing means of repression. The end of the world as predicted by the Orthodox priest, Father Maximos, appeared a real possibility. Another prediction, made by the eminent western scientist and father of Physics, Isaac Newton, also seemed to confirm this. It was said that just prior to his death, he jotted down that the end of the world would come in 2060. This year was therefore chosen by a cabal of the world's dominant powers to proclaim the imposition of the "Triptych System", which remains in power as I write.

Ion of the Sewer

AFTERWORD I have written the brief survey above following requests from many friends and fellow-citizens who, owing to their age, have not had the opportunity to follow the developments we have lived through during this century. I was born at the end of the twentieth century. I am over seventy years of age and have decided to impart certain details that explain how we have been led to the situation in which we now find ourselves. This is knowledge that many inhabitants have never had the opportunity to learn at school. I shall continue for as long as I can to provide more information to whoever asks me for it.

In the meantime, I will describe conditions in the place where I am now living. I am working with my shoulder leaning against the "wall". Beside me, almost touching me, a woman is cooking for her two children, who are playing a metre from us. There is a strong smell of metallic paint, inhaled by many inhabitants of the Sewer as a drug; all around me loud music blares from the recesses. These are the smells and sound encountered when one enters the basement of this city-state through the large hole in the city's main street. Small lamps are scattered along its tunnels and the same dance music can be heard everywhere. "If there is a club in Hell", a friend once said, "It must be something like this." - like these never-ending tunnels, as tortuous as the tentacles of an octopus, beneath the once superb capital of Bucharest. Not far away, half-naked people are squatting in a row, their bodies a mass of tattoos and scars; there are cats and dogs, and other tunnels leading to other spaces. Most of the residents come from the orphanages that have closed down. Despite our degradation, we do not believe we are the scum of society, rats or prisoners. It is the System which has flushed us out as if we were vomit. People come here, as they do in many other underground cities that have been created in Europe and America, for a little food, warmth and advice, looking for some protection. Because I have to say that it is only here that we are safe from persecution. It is only here in the sewers that it is impossible for the defenders to hunt us down. The limitations of this underground place and its narrow tunnels are incompatible with their specifications. It is impossible for them to move, to receive orders from the Centre and to transmit information back. So, we at least have some peace. The tuberculosis everywhere in the Sewer is a continuous threat but not as immediate as that posed by the defenders.

Ion of the Sewer

• • •

Klara, stunned, lifted her head. Reading was a rare activity for her. When everything can be done with electronics and holographs, writing is considered, not only today but for many years now, an almost medieval activity. It was not only the effort that made her head spin, however, it was also the content of the text. She would have said that she was in shock if she had been able to take it all in. But that was still impossible, since her experiences of life until now were in such contrast to what she had just read. Like day and night, she thought. How was it possible for the things she had just read about to belong to the same world in which, for as long as she could remember, she had been completely protected from every threat? How could she reconcile Ion's wretched life in the Sewer with the artificial needs and so-called problems that preoccupied the energies of people outside in the free atmosphere? How to understand the sufferings of those marginalized people when it was enough for her to show the irises of her eyes to her personal "Logic" card in order to have anything she wanted? In her world the only things that concerned her were the music of Duke Ellington, the imagined dangers of a recurrence of conjunctivitis, Lex Arlington's sex-life and the story of Hawaian shirts. How was it possible that there were people living in the conditions described by Ion down in the Sewer? How human were people down there? And how human are we up here? She added this last thought as she struggled to make sense of the emotions that had overwhelmed her from the reading. "And how human are we, when we know what is going on down there?"

5

ASHDAY

"How often will I have to compromise my principles in order to achieve my goal?" Michos wondered as the air-car flew over Asia Minor. Behind him the first rays of the sun were breaking up the darkness between the grey mountain peaks. "I'll have to make compromises," he corrected himself, "Simply to have some hope of achieving it. Simply some hope."

"Is it worth it?"He wondered. "Is it worth putting Alison at risk for something like that? And after so many years, years when we never had a single opportunity to meet....Of course...I've also involved Kamel in this venture. He said himself that the future for his family looks only bleak now. Any hope for them is fading. He said, after all, that he didn't care about his own future if it means having the opportunity to resist. Of course, I've also thrown the Indian and his Chinese friend into the fire I lit. They, at least, live in a separate world, where the accepted rules of the System seem to have been forgotten." He could find excuses for all his actions over the past days, actions whose one common characteristic was that he was breaking his own rules. The rules he had defined as the moral guidelines for his life, the first of which was never to cause harm to anyone. This basic principle had a value for him equivalent to his own life. "But now what have I done?" he thought, "I've put in danger the one and only person I've ever loved. The only person I would never want to come to harm." The regrets that had been tormenting him for some hours reached an unbearable climax with the fact that Alison had done nothing to avoid the catastrophe that her beloved was preparing for her. Not one 'No', not a single hesitant attempt to avoid the meeting that he had asked for after so many years. Not one pretext or procrastination. She had eagerly accepted his brief message. And the System, without yet knowing the details, had undoubtedly already noted, beyond his own 'transgression', another new and incomprehensible message to a member of society with Alison's status.

The air-car left him at the stop for the last Asian town, Ayvalik. From there he took a sea-taxi to Kydonies on the east coast of Mytilene. It was midday when he arrived at the place where they had spent the last moments of their love so many years ago; the place that their messages should not mention by name to avoid the location for their present meeting being detected. "The place which will become the location for my ex-love's downfall," Michos thought with strangely bitter determination as he stepped from the sea-taxi onto the quay. Leaving aside his regrets was assisted by the System's golden rule to its citizens. Among the orders given, using every available means - visual, electronic, holographic and audio – to be securely fixed in the scrambled subconscious of the masses was the fundamental rule for peace and calm in society: "Don't think about it!"

He walked towards the monastery. This was where they had been when they received the order from the System to separate. Their meeting place. He now vividly remembered how happy they had been on that visit to Lesvos and their discussions about the island's history. Alison, always proud of her Indian roots and with a strong desire to help her tribe's revival, was interested in any similar preservation of old traditions. Here on this island she found that great religious and political changes were always accompanied by some reconciliation with tradition, even if only temporary, and that had held her interest for the duration of the visit, until their sudden separation. The day before, they had been at a village for a religious festival, the festival of Saint George. Here, as elsewhere, a custom from pagan times had been preserved. On the eve of the festival, a bullock would be chosen for sacrifice and taken to the church to be blessed by the priest. The following day, a procession with the bullock and men on horseback would make a round of the village accompanied by musicians, locals, devotees and other visitors who scattered flowers along the road to the centre of the village. Here a sort of auction took place to raise money for the ritual, which continued throughout the night. Alison and Michos had attended this festival and afterwards visited the church of Saint Rafael, famous for its splendid murals. It was there that they had received the heartbreaking order from the System to separate.

As he walked up the hill, Michos thought that his visit today to the same church was an unexpected opportunity to see whether the old conviction about the difficulty the area was having in passing from one religion to another was, even now, very much alive. A number of years ago, the major religions were disbanded and the only one still permitted was the so-called Neutral Religion. This had first appeared in Berlin, Germany, where the first place was built for Christians, Jews and Muslims to worship together. It was named "The House of One". There had been declarations both in favour and against this innovation. However, those in favour won since it was considered that such a solution, on a wider scale, would rein in and then end the uncontrollable outbreaks of violence and even massacres that had occurred in the intervening years, before the imposition of the Triptych System. One leading imam's declaration at the time had greatly helped the Neutral Religion to be accepted. He, together with other important religious figures, had said that, "The House of One" would be a message to the world that the great majority of Muslims are peace-loving and non-violent. Thousands of others quickly followed the "House of One", allowing the Triptych System to decisively limit the worship of other religions with smaller followings. To facilitate this development, the "House of One" was designed with each religion on a different level, featuring holy areas and a place for Muslims to wash their feet. The institution as a whole was characterized by an all-embracing "balanced" absence. There was no minaret or belfry. "It was logical", those in power had said then, "Since those features were aimed at propagating the public face of each religion and hence encouraging fanaticism. Each 'House of One' contained a fourth room. This was destined for use by people who did not belong to one of the three religions or by those without any faith."

When Michos reached the church entrance he saw that the door was closed. He tried the handle. He smiled as he thought that, here too, old customs were kept alive for a much longer time, before being cast aside and replaced by new ones. The door yielded and he immediately found himself in the familiar space. In the riot of colour that he remembered. Vivid colours, scenes depicting historical and traditional scenes of Christianity since its birth, on the walls, the pillars, the semi-circle of the dome and the passageways of the church. He smiled with relief. He was not especially religious. It gave him pleasure, however, to think that here and there traditions had refused to disappear; that the Neutral Religion steamroller had not managed to reach every corner of the world. The prospect of Alison reacting with similar enthusiasm also gave him pleasure.

He came out of the Church and saw her silhouette at the far end of the path, approaching with her familiar walk, with a spring in every step. He had been right to think for so many years that whoever came close to her could never forget her. That certainly applied to him. She entered his dreams every night, sometimes to couple with him in a frenzy of eroticism; at other times with a serious demeanour, the one needed when exercising the duties of leader of her tribe. He always wondered: would he have been happier after their forced separation if he had completely forgotten her, if he had become reconciled to

70

the monotony of his life, if he had felt the abandonment profoundly until his death or if he had kept, as now, the memory of her alive and the wound of separation still open?

She was now close and he could see the beginning of a smile on her lips. Wearing a brown tracksuit, half her face was in sunlight while the rest was in shadow as if to emphasise the duality of her temperament. A thick, jet-black plait hung over her shoulder and across her right breast, a plait she had the habit of holding in her hand so that it didn't bother her as she walked. The smile on her lips had spread to her whole face as she stopped two paces away from Michos. But the expression in her eyes remained calm and solemn, like black fire.

"Welcome!" he said awkwardly.

"Welcome to you, too, from our other life!" Amsey, motionless, she looked in his eyes and then at his arms. Were they going to open in welcome?

He embraced her eagerly. He pressed his face against her cheek.

Without thinking he whispered, "Will you ever forgive me for the disaster I've caused you?" As if believing his question required an answer.

"You'll need to forgive me more than I need to forgive you," she replied. "Let's go into the church. Out here there isn't a place on earth that isn't watching us."

"How have all these managed to survive?" Amsey wondered in amazement as her gaze filled with the dazzling colours of the murals. I thought that around the mid-century they'd all been destroyed, together with everything they stood for."

Michos did not reply. He thought how he had correctly predicted the reaction of his past love. "Was it past?" He wondered.

"It seems, Alison, that during the conflicts there were exceptions which survived," he said.

"Amsey, call me Amsey," she murmured. "After my transformation I decided to turn back to my tribe. In theory I am still their representative, don't forget."

"Amsey, then. What happened to make you change ....?"

"What stopped happening and made me change would be a better question..."

"I'm sorry; I didn't mean to be tactless..."

"I changed it as soon as I stopped being the System's plaything, if you know what I mean. As soon as I was again given a job which, although perhaps not worth much, at least is not the disgusting life that I was forced to live in the first years."

"I didn't want..."Michos tried to interrupt her.

"You don't want, but I want to tell you. I'm not the same person that I was all those years ago. And I don't want to remember what I did then, nor what my name was when I was taking orders from whichever leading figure in politics or the economy I had to sleep with every night."

"Don't...please," Michos turned, and took her hands. He looked her in the eyes, almost begging her to stop the painful confession.

"I'm telling you because I want you to know that you are no longer speaking to the girl you once loved."

He looked at her even harder. "And whom I've always loved and will always love." His voice was low but under the colourful sunlit dome it sounded like thunder. "Come and sit down. We have to talk." They sat on one of the church benches and he began to explain his reasons for breaking every rule for her security, and the plan of action he had drawn up over the last few days. He told her about grandfather Mihalis' discovery, about his attempt to find people with the right know-how, about his hopes for the success of the scheme and his disappointment when one of them had told him that access to a gold "Logic" card was essential for getting the intended messages to the right people. "Without it," he ended, "All the dangers we have been exposed to will have been for nothing."

"Now at least you understand that my motives for choosing you were not entirely selfish...."

"Did you perhaps choose me because you wanted to see me again?" she murmured. Michos did not understand whether her question was playful or hid a hope frustrated through the years.

• • •

After the acts of terrorism against European and Asian nuclear power stations, nuclear power had gradually fallen into disuse and to replace this lost energy the T.S. had constructed two enormous dams which regulated but also lowered water levels in the western and eastern Mediterranean, thus producing huge amounts of electricity and supplying the whole of Europe. It had been an old idea from the early days of Nazism in the first decades of the twentieth century, aimed at uniting Europe with its twin dogma of colonization and nationalism. The project, for obvious reasons, had not been given the name thought up by the Nazis, "Atlantropa", with its dual reference to Atlantis and Europe, but had been realized on the same basic plans of the previous century and was a complete success.

These changes had also affected the coast near Mytilene's Petrified Forest. The bay, one of many new bays created throughout the Archipelago, extended over hundreds of metres and small cabins had been constructed there for tourists. It was in one of these that Michos and Amsey spent their few hours together. There they renewed their former intimacy, and with eyes closed and her head on his chest, she silently wept and he did not ask the reason for her grieving. She was thankful for his silence and he tenderly caressed her long black mane of hair. There they were able to forget the bitter and endless years of separation and feel again the extraordinary spiritual lightness that accompanied their every union, even more intensely on this particular evening.

A discussion Michos had had with Babar and Su Dong just a few hours earlier was returning constantly to his thoughts. Su maintained that, apart from the conscious state and the dream state, there is a third one, somewhere in between. It is the one that features in certain Asian traditions, whose cultures recognize the existence of the so-called lucid dreams. Or, paradoxically, the latent ability of an individual to direct consciousness and to produce dreams at will. These dreams are considered a significant part of the lives of people who find themselves between sleep and the awakened state; a state which may be useful in the production of conscious dreams capable of curing various ailments. Michos felt that this moment in his life belonged in that category. That it was a lucid dream. He remembered words from the past he had once written, inspired by a certain poet:

"I will have a dream,
That I love you in a dream
And into your soul I will dive deeply,
Into the abyss of your dark eyes,
In the tresses of your jet-black mane of hair
And I will stay silent and motionless with fear
That I may shatter both us and our dreams."

He had whispered these words into her ear when it was still night and she was curled up in his arms.

"Is it still there? The dream?" Amsey asked. She had spent the hours trying to banish everything she had lived through, everything she had learned and done over the years of her enforced "service" to the System. She had tried to be the same young girl who had met the beloved man in the time when her love was spontaneous. That was the appropriate word for this night, she thought, "spontaneous". Perhaps it was her last chance to be spontaneous in this life. Even more, perhaps this chance, being the last, was something for which she should be grateful in the light of her fate. "Is it still there?" she asked again. "The dream? But yes. The dream is you, it is me, and it is both of us. Didn't you see it clearly tonight?"

"You're right." Amsey pressed herself more closely against his chest. "Do you have other dreams? They are part of your character after all…"

"Do you believe there's no point to them?" Michos brought his mouth close to her lips. "I believe they are necessary…because without them a person cannot hope for any sort of better life."

"To think that we allowed ourselves to trust the great scientific discoveries of the past without bothering to connect them to some form of essential humanitarianism. What happened benefitted industries, made a small number of business people rich, brought catastrophe to whole populations, and led to the foundation of today's System, which leaves no room for freedom and has become a global and uncontrolable power. Without some sort of aim or dream, how can anything happen for us to live like human beings again?"

Amsey remained silent for a long time. Then, gently,

"Do you believe you can bring about a revolution with just a few collaborators?"

"I believe that revolutions by large numbers of armed citizens have no hope whatsoever of success. The measures that were first used for the security of the majority have led to the control of our every move, even our every thought, by the central power, forbidding any action outside the imposed modes of behavior. I believe that, since the traditional form of revolution is doomed to failure, there has to be another kind that can succeed. Today, weapons would be our downfall. Today, it's knowledge that is needed, not only for us but also for those in power, for our lives to be made better."

"That's how Eliot put it in the mid-twentieth century," she whispered in his ear: "Where is the wisdom we have lost in knowledge? Where is the knowledge we have lost in information?"

They remained silent for a long time. Until they decided the moment had come for Amsey to leave and make the copy of Hassan Porter's gold "Logic" card.

"I still have something to tell you, not in the words of a famous poet, though," she whispered, "But in the words of an unknown, eastern shaman that give me the strength for what I'm about to do."

"If you want to change the world, love a man. Love him truly." She said goodbye with a lingering kiss.

• • •

Hassan Porter began his career in perfect circumstances for the time. His father – a moderate Muslim – had distanced himself from the religious disputes of his adolescence. When he married, he was careful to pass on to his son Hassan the same moderate views on religion. Views in line with his own. So it came about that his son was able, at the right moment, to demonstrate convincingly that he was one of the still few followers of the Neutral Religion. This decision helped Hassan to speedily ascend the ladder of the Triptych System's hierarchy, particularly when he chose to follow his specialization at the Higher School of Communication Politics in Paris. He found himself there at a time when French culture was being radically transformed. After the changes in principles that had occurred mid-century and the religious conflicts, many people, as had often occurred in that country's history, turned their sights to the only apparently peaceful solution to their problems: the adoption of Neutral Religion. This, together with his specialization in communications, qualified Hassan for a life's work which not only gave him professional satisfaction but promoted him quickly to the top echelons of international power.

Within ten years of the founding of the Triptych System, he had become one of its foremost communications experts and every Administrative body paid him handsomely for his advice. Hassan had the capability of separating news into multiple categories, to analyse these in exhaustive detail, to remove everything that might create the slightest anxiety, causing all suggestion of danger for the public to disappear, while promoting to the heavens any piece of pleasing and refreshing news. Finally, he could build whole narratives of news upon the slightest indication of anything, bringing to life a general, almost horizontal, spirit of well-being in a world where the young, at least, had never known the meaning of individuality.

News construction was indeed Hassan Porter's specialization, a specialization which of course had its dangers for someone without his abilities. These abilities had given him the advantage of being one of very few peers never accused of unsuccessful falsification of news, together with his particular skill in the zero production of news in the service of the Triptych System. Moreover, the activities, through holographic presentation, of the most celebrated journalist couple of the day were his creation. This creation had brought hundreds of millions to his bank accounts and continued to make him richer by the day. Indeed, the daily global broadcast by "Tito and Titi" was eagerly awaited by millions of viewers. What they presented was blindly absorbed by a great part of global opinion, whose reactions thus had the advantage of being within the desired range of limits for the System to continue operating smoothly. Tito and Titi had become not only the template for information but also the idols of an adoring younger generation, and were to be found in electronic productions, entertaining adventures, children's games as well as fictional series.

Hassan Porter created and was also responsible for the publication of a weekly holographic magazine, which constituted the semi-official organ of global governmental guidance. It was here the Triptych System outlined policy with regard to population reduction, successes in the struggle against a vague source of impending terrorism, general reassurance of the citizenry, the satisfactory incomes policy and the benefits of the now widespread genetically modified foods when compared with natural foods, which in any case were not only almost impossible to find but whose use was forbidden. Hassan's success in the field of propaganda stemmed from his knowledge of neuroscience. He knew very well how to direct the intense activity of his messages towards the prefrontal cortex of his listener-viewers' brains, so that the promotional message would be stored in his human targets' long-term memories.

As he meditated on brain-related matters, the picture of Klara came to mind and he smiled to himself. Here was a case in point where there was no chance of influence, he thought. Here was a case where exerting the influence of his advanced knowledge and all those scientific seminars was unnecessary. A simple, horizontal and problem-free female brain, whose only preoccupations were enjoyment, luxury, games and love-making. Love-making for which, to be honest, Hassan recognised that Klara had a special talent. Although he suspected that this was partly due to the female supervisor, Amsey, assigned to her by the System. A very beautiful but also mysterious woman. He brushed the thought aside. Mysteries held no attraction for him. They repelled him and he took care that other people should avoid them too. This was his work. The beautiful Indian gave the impression of not following the path of "common opinion". And common opinion was of primary concern to his role in society. It was his life's aim to shape it and for there to be no scope for anyone to move outside it.

Klara appeared at that moment. Her appearance was, as always, sublime. With her perfect body, alluring walk and dazzling smile, she dismissed his dark thoughts like a breath of fresh air. She approached and gave him a warm kiss. Her flimsy, loose-fitting garment brushed against him and was enough to arouse him. He went to hold her but she clearly first wished to prepare their union more carefully. She drew herself up and began to make slow dance-like movements to some pre-programmed eastern music. Hassan felt pleasure, he enjoyed her with his eyes and suddenly the erotic tension spread to all his senses. He got up, took hold of her and made love to her on the sofa, more forcefully than in a long time.

After some time, Klara got up and, as if unwilling to accept that their evening had come to an end, as if she had not yet had the satisfaction that her young body desired, began again to sway, now naked – Hassan, having hurled her diaphanous garment to the floor in the heat of the moment. He shuddered again. To increase the desire he felt, he picked up the control for the holographic transmitter and pressed the button repeatedly. The large room filled with holographic copies of Klara, who followed the swaying of their prototype. It was now a space packed with incredibly beautiful women, a space with such a myriad of holographic women that Hassan was unable to tell which of the alluring dancers the real one was. Klara and her lookalikes suddenly stopped: it became a room of motionless naked women. Hassan stretched out his arms but saw something different in her eyes, something indicating resentment.

"Is anything wrong?" he asked. Klara did not reply. She lowered her eyes and gathered her garment from the floor.

"Tell me what's wrong?" insisted Hassan. Klara did not speak, her head still bowed. "Keep calm!" she thought. "Remember how fortunate you are. Think what others go through who don't have it."

But Hassan was getting angry. He grabbed her by the shoulders, stared her in the eyes and shouted, "Tell me what's going on!"

The tears that welled up did not stop him. On the contrary they made him even angrier. He shook her furiously.

"What's going on?" He shouted.

A whole range of accumulated emotions prevented Klara from understanding at that moment what made her respond to her lover's pressure.

"Look!" she faltered, "I waited so many days for you to come and see me, for us to enjoy something together ...". She paused. "And when you do come, it's as if you see me through a hologram. Like an electric doll..."

"You don't appreciate what I do for you", replied Hassan heatedly. "You should be more aware of what you've got, thanks to me, and what others don't have. Others who not even in their dreams...."

"I do know what others don't have..." she blurted out.

"You have no idea!" he shouted at her.

"I do know. I know that there are people who live like animals in the sewers..."

Hassan stared at her, speechless. "It's the fault of that Indian bitch," he thought, "She's opened Klara's eyes. I'll take care of her, but right now I must stay calm."

Without another word, he got up and went to the bedroom. "I'm going to sleep!" he called out and lay down without paying her any further attention.

"Women!" He thought, fixing his eyes on the domed ceiling above the bed to which Klara had not accompanied him.

The Neutral Religion, as a combination of compromises between the extremes of earlier religions, had erased certain of their particular characteristics which had served as pretexts for religious conflict. Among these was the disappearance of belfries and minarets. There remained however a number of things which had sometimes benefitted both the former Christian faith and Islam. In the second category was the general prohibition against eating pork and society's negative treatment of women. With the great reforms of the Neutral Religion, the System noted that women were regaining the privileged position they had enjoyed in society under the earlier regime, and was taking measures to limit it. Hassan, despite being a moderate, accepted that, indeed, the treatment of women did have to be more strictly regulated than before. "This evening's events have justified such a viewpoint," he thought as he fell asleep.

6

CHROMEDAY

The first glint of sunlight had triumphantly broken through in the east when Amsey boarded Klara's floating villa. She was armed with Babar's mnemonema to do what she had promised Michos: to copy all the memory of Hassan's gold "Logic" card. When she reached the main lounge of the vessel, she was puzzled to find Klara asleep on a sofa instead of at the side of her beloved in the big bedroom. In vain she glanced around the room in the hope of seeing something that would help her to understand what had happened. She approached Klara and woke her as gently as she could. The unexpected change, together with the limited time at her disposal made the task she had undertaken for Michos now seem impossible. Klara, still drowsy, explained in general terms what had happened the previous evening and Hassan's anger. "He's in the bedroom and asleep, I think." She whispered. "You have to go to him right now," answered Amsey, hurriedly. "All your future depends on this one act of yours."

"I don't know....after what happened yesterday..." whined Klara.

"Go right now! For your own good. And it would be better if he doesn't wake up when you get in beside him. So he has a pleasant surprise when he wakes up," she said, giving Klara a wink. She helped her to get up and accompanied her to the entrance of bedroom.

She waited some time and, not hearing any noise or the sound of them speaking, she slipped into the bedroom so quietly that even her Navajo ancestors would have been envious of her. She knew from Hassan's previous visits exactly where he left his personal items when he slept with Klara. Lying on her back on the floor beside the bed, she stretched out her arm to the bedside table and felt for the "Logic" card that Hassan had placed next to him. She passed the "Mnemonema" into the slot and waited patiently for several minutes until the copy had been made. Silently, she then placed the card back in exactly the same position and left the room. Satisfied that despite the unexpected setback, her task had been successful.

Hassan Porter had a pleasant awakening. As he turned, his arm touched the smooth skin of Klara's body. He opened his eyes and, as always, his first move was to kiss her full, half-open, lips. With his passion violently aroused, Hassan embraced her and their two bodies quickly became one. His desire and their morning encounter made the evening disappointment another reason for them to enjoy the union more intensely. Klara's orgasm was so unrestrained that for a moment it had frightened Hassan. But it ended in the wonderful calm that always enveloped them after loving. Lying on his back, Hassan smiled. Finally, yesterday evening's episode did not mean anything. He had to forget all about it. But he needed to make sure that it did not occur again. With this aim in mind, he had thought of using two means. First of all to give his sweet Klara a good lesson, to explain what life was really like "out there" so that she would not be influenced by irresponsible rumours; and second to make sure that miserable Indian woman who had had such a bad influence on her life should be made to disappear.

He closed his eyes and planned, as he did so often, the word and moves he would used to instruct Klara correctly. He did the same thing every time he prepared an important move in his work - in his work of influencing the public. For this reason, Hassan reckoned with great certainty that his words would persuade Klara in the end that, whatever she thought, her life was a rare case of good fortune, a privilege, and that she must not have a single thought for those who did not have her good luck. The "I" is "I", and the "other" is the "other". To think with the logic of solidarity is not only unreasonable and outdated but also dangerous.

· · ·

One last embrace. Michos thought about the word "last".

"I want us to meet as soon as this crisis has passed." He spoke quietly into her ear.

"So do I." She did not add what she knew only too well. That it would be impossible after the previous day they had spent together.

"You don't sound sure," said Michos rather foolishly. "For me to be sure, I'd have to have no knowledge of how the system works. But I do know. I assure you."

"We can hope, though. In any case, they might not be able to read our messages using the code of your tribe."

"Perhaps," replied Amsey, and her kiss was more like an act of spiritual abandonment.

One of Klara's cloned puppies which had just received its annual vaccine, came by itself and accompanied her to the beach. Despite the mist clouding Michos' gaze, he managed to follow the figures of the woman and dog until they boarded the small boat.

· · ·

The one-time tourist guest houses of Camp number 425 were full of people who, as far as Nora could make out, all had something in common.

83

A characteristic though which she could not yet determine. Normally, in a prison – because Camp 425 was essentially a prison – there should be all types and all ages of people whose only common factor would be their transgression of the law. But in the Camp the male and female in-mates were aged between twenty and forty or children with their adult parents and almost no elderly people at all. There was only one elderly woman whose daughter looked after her and who had become the attraction of Nora's wing. Not only because she was the only person in the Camp who was enthusiastic about her accommodation and the fact that she was frequently heard to exclaim, "Ooooopa, ooooopa!" as if she were back in a youthful dream dancing; but also because she insisted that her daughter spoon feed her with her soup at every meal, and then would bite on the spoon and stubbornly refuse to let go of it.

"Don't bite on the spoon!" Her daughter would shout at her. But the old lady would not let it go, believing that it was the only way to ensure her daily food.

In the same wing as Nora there was also a man in his forties from Montenegro, Vlado, who had introduced himself to her as an aeronautical engineer. He was a tall, very attractive man. He spoke with the appearance of calm but betrayed an underlying anxiety. When Nora asked him what his job had been before ending up in the Camp, Vlado hesitated. As if he was making an effort to hold back the anger that was welling up inside him.

"I was a leading expert in the construction of rockets. As to how I find myself here...." He stopped.

"I wasn't asking about that," Nora hastily replied, "Although I can certainly tell you why I am here. They have accused me of religious proselytizing... Something I know absolutely nothing about."

"I am here for something I possess exclusively professionally and technically." He replied, and his grey eyes now looked fiery. He stopped for a moment to keep his cool. "If I were not one of the most successful aeronautical engineers I would not have been accused of selling secrets to so-called anarchists."

"A serious charge," Nora let the comment slip out.

"And as baseless as the charge against you. The thing is that while I don't think the people in the System need anyone to practise religion proselytizing in the Camp...on the contrary, they have a desperate need for someone with my specialization for what they want from us." In answer to the enquiring look he received from Nora, Vlado said, "You must have heard something. You must have...although you arrived only recently..."

Seeing she did not respond, he decided not to continue the conversation, which would only add problems to those she already had. He only asked, "Who accused you of wanting to proselytize?"

"A neighbour. She did not hide the fact that she is a Muslim and the only comment I made to her was that for her own good she should not be so open. That was all and she, instead of thanking me, went and reported me for wanting to change her religious convictions. Without saying of course that she herself was not a follower of the Neutral Religion. That's how I've ended up here..."

Vlado shook his head. "They need families, too." In answer to Nora's puzzled expression, he decided to explain what he meant.

"It's about a big programme that started many years ago. I'm talking about the one called 'Persephone'."

"I've heard about it."

"It's a big space mission with thousands of passengers. Of course they need directly related specializations such as my own, but also many others who will enrich the population that will be settled on the distant planet to create a colony of earthlings."

"You mean..."Nora dared not believe what she had understood from the words of her new friend.

"I mean that all of us here at the Camp are candidates for a sort of selection that will take place to man the spacecraft."

"And if those they select don't agree?"

"They will agree in some way or will be forced to agree. Mainly, though, they will be persuaded through the control of sleep-education

85

already in use. It won't only remove the fears of those selected for the big journey but is also going to persuade them that they are taking part in a humanitarian mission aimed at the salvation of the Earth from future catastrophe and other similar excuses. Unconsciously, all the candidates will have been persuaded that they have a dazzling future and that each through his own contribution will save mankind." Vlado's face with difficulty hid the bitter irony of his words.

Nora froze. The reason was not so much the general information Vlado was giving her at that moment. It was what one of her two sons, Marios, had told her the past two days. He was a sensitive child with many gifts and a wide range of interests; a child who stood out at school for his knowledge and who always showed kindness and concern for others. Marios had described to her the strange dreams he had had the past two nights. He had always found it easy to remember his dreams but it seemed that the ones he had described to Nora had a particular intensity about them. He had told her that in the beginning his dream had been full of obstacles, dangers and delusions. Later, in the same dream things unfolded with the fading away of dangers and particularly pleasant moments. They finished with arrival at some majestic city in the sky. It was so beautiful that waking up was unbearably distressing. The child had confessed to his mother that straight after waking he had tried to go back to sleep to feel again and again the delight of his wonderful journey.

"I have to inform Kamel immediately," thought Nora as she went along the central road through the Camp looking for her husband. He had isolated himself in the café outside the Camp gates and was searching his "Logic" card desperately for some details which, as he had told his wife, a colleague had requested. As she walked with her thoughts focused on Marios' dream, her mind suddenly lit up with one of her own; the dream she had had the previous night: There was a drop of water that had fallen in the palm of her hand. As she looked more closely at it, she suddenly saw that it was growing, becoming a very beautiful transparent ball in which she found herself. The ball

grew and grew and became enriched with gardens, rivers and mountain tops, each more beautiful than the one before. Her senses became
aware of the sound of running water everywhere, of cool air caressing
her hair and gentle music complementing the perfection of the place,
which seemed to have been given to her as a gift to enjoy. It had been
a joy which she too had felt deprived of by waking up.

At the gate, she asked one of the guards who happened to be leaving the Camp at that moment to inform Kamel that his wife needed
to speak to him. A few minutes later, seated on a bench, she recounted
to her husband everything Vlado had told her as well as the dreams
his son and she had had.

• • •

On the other side of the Camp, Vlado was watching a programme of
Central Holographic Information with great interest. The reason for
his interest was that for the first time an official announcement was
being made about the forthcoming mission being planned by the T.S.
to the planet of Mars. The programme was being presented by Tito
and Titi.

The two presenters were saying very convincingly that the main
aim of the mission would be to create the right conditions for the establishment in due course of a colony consisting of some tens of thousands of people on the planet which, to apparently meet the needs of
the presentation, was not referred to as the "Red Planet" as in the past,
but the "Dream Planet". "It's a neologism to avoid discouraging the
new travelers," thought Vlado. Since, as the two presenters confirmed,
the first settlers would be volunteers and naturally would be perfectly
prepared and well-informed for what they would find on the great
journey. The aim of this first, serious endeavour was to transfer the
suitable engineering equipment and install domes made inhabitable
with oxygen. At the same time, work would be carried out to create
the necessary conditions for the cultivation of the ground before the

main consignment of people was settled. The Planet was presented as a great opportunity for the inhabitants of Earth to find plentiful sources of energy and incalculable riches. To create, in other words, conditions with limitless natural sources thus securing the survival of our ageing planet, Earth, for many centuries to come.

There followed various pieces information about the cost of the programme, the specializations that volunteer candidates should have, their age, the ways scientists had used in order to guarantee the safety of the mission, from the time of the journey up to the way of life inside the spaceship which would transport them given that this transportation would last.... etc. etc.

Vlado watched the programme to the end and his first thought when it ended was to find Nora and tell her what he had found out. It was telling that this was the first official presentation that had been made by the System. Up to now there had been only rumours. But now it was official. Regarding the System's assurance that the mission would be manned exclusively by volunteers, Vlado had his doubts. His own case was enough to make him disbelieve it.

Someone else, far away from Vlado and the environment of the Camp had followed the same programme with even stronger emotions. He was particularly satisfied with the presentation because he had been its creator. Hassan Porter, seated in the armchair in Klara's lounge had, with professional dedication throughout the programme, tried to detect any faults. To his satisfaction, he ascertained that there had been nothing worthy of criticism. At least by anyone without specialized knowledge. Today was a good day for him, he concluded. He had sold a campaign to the T.S. which would run for years and would secure yet another fortune for him. He had proved to Klara once again his prowess in erotic performance. And finally, he had shaken off the disastrous influence of that wretched Indian woman over Klara, who was now lying on her own sofa, exhausted by the erotic pleasure he had bestowed upon her.

7

PLUMDAY

The gentle waves were a pleasant distraction from Amsey's thoughts as she headed for Klara's impressive floating palace in her small boat. Opposite her, behind the ship, the densely inhabited coastline of Asia Minor was visible and at intervals other ships appeared carrying their cargoes in all directions. She had just left the coast of Mytilene, and Michos. She knew that the previous day was the last with him that she would remember. Her fate was now sealed. She did not know exactly when, but it was inevitable that something unpleasant would happen to her very soon. Her fears were realised while she was still some distance from Klara's floating palace. Two hovercraft-like power-boats arrived at high speed and forced her to stop. Two defenders in one of the boats indicated with their electronic eyes that she should not move. Within a couple of minutes they had taken her aboard and then both boats set off towards the Asian coastline. Amsey looked back sadly at her little craft left drifting between the island and Klara's yacht. Anyone looking for her – Klara for example – would assume she had been taken out to sea. She would soon be forgotten. Just then, one of the defenders placed an adhesive blindfold over her eyes.

Some time later, she realised that she was in one of those places called "sterilizers" by those who had the misfortune of experiencing them at first-hand. These were places where visitors were stripped of every secret they might have acquired in the course of their lives, every personal memory and whatever might indicate even the slightest trace of individuality. They left that place – if they left at all, of course – purged, drained of every personal burden of which the System did not approve and with every misdemeanor, whether real or imagined, expunged.

A mechanical voice spoke. It came from deep inside Amsey's ear. Clearly the adhesive blindfold fulfilled another role. It conveyed verbal messages directly to her.

"Who did you meet two days ago at the petrified forest on Mytilene?" was the first question.

With this first question came the realization that the moment had arrived to test whether her tribe's values still existed and, moreover, whether she was capable of proving she could live up to the responsibilities of leadership that she had been true to all her life. She therefore decided that, at least in this first phase, she would refuse to answer.

"What relationship do you have with the person you met in Mytilene?" was the second question.

"What did this person confide in you during your meeting? What are his intentions?" The voice continued with no indication of impatience at the absence of any response.

"We know that he is planning action that is categorized as terrorism. You may confide the information to us that will enable us to thwart this action. Alternatively, you will be considered to share responsibility and will suffer the same consequences as the perpetrator", the metallic voice continued.

The voice was not new to Amsey. She had often heard it when she was a member of the team putting together the programme for the promotion of the huge "Ten Years" anniversary celebrations of the T.S. The System suspected that many people were not in agreement with all that had come about during that ten-year period and so two Defenders had been detailed to the team to deal with any reactionary activity.

She could picture them, there was no need to open her eyes: short, robot-like, with a hexagonal head, two cold yellow eyes and a third red one in the centre that was different; with a square mouth that opened and shut as it spoke to her, reeling off its questions.

Its manner, it seemed to Amsey, did not bode well. She knew that it was now standing close to her and she felt a small jab of pain in her arm. Defenders were programmed to perform other duties apart from those of policing. For instance, the implanting of a tracker which used radio frequencies, better known as an RFID, which this particular defender had just hypodermically implanted in her. This was the critical event which turned Amsey into a direct component of the System. Over and above all the data on her "Logic" card and her exact location on Earth at any given moment, it contained her DNA and every financial detail of her existence.

Immediately following this, the same sequence of questions was repeated: "Who did you meet two days ago at the Petrified Forest ....?" The defenders were clearly prepared to give her a little more time to answer. Amsey knew what would be next. The defenders would have to request permission for this. Permission to use their most persuasive means of making her give them the answers they expected. She knew that this was their third, red, eye. The eye that nobody could forget. Because it was this that administered pain.

So now Amsey had to prepare herself to endure pain. The right place for her was not where she found herself today, she thought. The right place was within her so-called "primitive" society, with the Navajo. One of those societies, that is, which had effectively held out against the other, supposedly progressive, societies that had robbed the "primitive" ones of everything they had. The latter's resistance had ensured their survival up to the moment when they ceased to resist. As long as they had remained "primitive" they survived, but when they decided, or were forced, to adapt to the progressive societies, they disappeared. Amsey's theory was that it had been their primitive nature that had saved them. And that the missionaries they opened their doors to had gradually made them strangers in their own natural world, finally destroyed by "progress" in their own forests. With this thought of the ethical supremacy of her age-old tradition, she disconnected all sensation and energy from her body. She used the method taught her by the tribe. She felt her energy drop to such a point of exhaustion that she became detached from her material being, from her own body. And at that exact moment, when she felt ready to receive the torture from the defender's red eye, she felt a burning sensation penetrating her right breast. "Strange," she thought, "The burning is not painful." One phrase remained with her for a long time, for the entire duration of the torture. A phrase that she repeated over and over: "The ancestors are here and are helping me", "The ancestors are here and are helping me", "The ancestors are here and are helping me".

• • •

Michos' return to the shack is now marked by a real explosion of energy from the whole team. Around the small table, shoulders almost touching, they are completing the preparation of the programme. Kamel is adding the quotations, rules and teachings from thousands of years of history, democracy, humanitarianism and culture. Michos is coordinating the requirements of the programme with Babar to achieve the desired result. Su Dong is helping by checking the links and provisions of the system prepared by Babar.

"I have an idea" Su says suddenly.

The others stop and look at her questioningly. "Do you know that a baby has vivid recall of the melodies it hears when in its mother's womb?"

The unexpected question causes the intense activity of the others to freeze.

"They have tested many applications of this phenomenon in the Chinese educational system. Music is used to a great extent, when necessary, for the most difficult part of learning our language, memorizing the characters," adds Su, raising her voice.

"You mean...?" "I mean that perhaps it would be a good idea to 'dress up' the knowledge that we want to transmit with music, which will make it easier to absorb and recognize. For it to be more firmly embedded in the human consciousness."

"I remember reading something," Kamel added. "Students, I think they were at some French university, got a number of pregnant women to listen to a certain piece of music for many weeks. After they had given birth, the researchers exposed the babies to the same music, together with another piece of music that they had not heard before. According to the results, the babies' heartbeats slowed down more when they listened to the 'familiar' music than when they listened to the other, unknown music. The researchers thus ascertained that the new-born babies paid greater attention and responded more to the music that their mothers had listened to."

The topic suddenly acquired interest for the team. Each one wanted to add some personal experience relating to the influence of music in education and the retention of knowledge by the memory. Su added that, according to the Chinese research, if mothers want to improve their children's sensitivity to music, they expose the child to music immediately after birth, when they can see what gives the child pleasure or otherwise - something they cannot know from the response of an embryo. And if the mother wishes to sing to the child, the result is even better. "The maternal song creates a wonderful natural sound environment for the baby."

"I don't imagine anyone is proposing that we should start singing to the rulers of the world to create a suitable environment..." Michos interjected, trying to bring the team back to their task.

"Of course not!" Kamel, despite all the pressure he was feeling, managed to smile. "Of course not! But if music improves a student's memory, I don't see why a specific type of music shouldn't help to imprint in the memories of leaders the thoughts, meanings and principles that are going to be valuable from now on for our fellow human beings." "It has a certain logic," admitted Michos. "But we haven't got time to prepare something like that. Our task now is for as much knowledge as possible to be loaded into the programme and to prepare the necessary parameters for transferring everything on to the "Logic" cards, and particularly the gold ones."

"Should we leave Su to take care of it?" Babar did not want his friend's idea to be forgotten.

"We'll leave her to it. But we can't be delayed by it," said Michos, and Kamel, worried about what was happening at the Purification Camp, indicated his agreement with a nod.

Michos bent over the table beside Kamel and became absorbed in following the dicta the Egyptian was then downloading from the mnemonema on to Babar's computer. They were flowing into the memory at great speed and he only had time to catch a few before they vanished into the infinite chaos of human knowledge: "Poverty is a virtue which one can teach oneself" (Diogenes, 410-323 BC Cynical philosopher); "There are four characteristics of perfect virtue: temperance, justice, courage and wisdom" (Plato 427 – 347 BC); "Human glory and riches end up in the soil, and all that and admiration for that is lost. Only the glory of virtue goes on forever" (Ioannis Chrysostomos 347-407 AD); "Virtue and wealth are rarely found in the same person" (Oscar Wilde, 1854-1900, Irish Writer); "Humility is the basis of all other virtues" (Confucius, 551-479 A.D.); "Ah! What is the point of being sunk in mud up to the neck and keeping your fingernails clean?" (Bertolt Brecht, 1898-1956, German writer); "Wherever power is concentrated in a few hands, it is certain that the people who have obtained power have the attitude of gangsters" (Lord Acton, 1834-1902, English historian); "When greed becomes a way of life for a group of people in a society, with the passage of time they will develop a legal system to legitimize it and an ethical code to reward it" (Frédéric Bastiat, 1801-1850, French economist); "Man's worst enemy is himself" (Anacharsis, 6th C. BC, Scythian leader and philosopher); "A man who has been socialized is far better than an animal. If however he distances himself from the law and the sense of justice, he becomes much worse than any animal" (Plato, 427-347 BC, Philosopher); "A man is the sum of his actions. Of what he has done, of what he can do. Nothing else." (Mahatma Gandhi, 1869-1948, Indian leader); "My father said there were two kinds of people in the world: Givers and takers. The takers may eat better, but the givers sleep better." (Marlo Thomas, 1937-, American actress & feminist). "Knowing what must be done does away with fear." (Rosa Parks of the Civil Rights Movement who refused to leave a bus seat designated 'For Whites').

There was such a volume of dicta entering Babar's computer that for the first time Michos felt overwhelmed by a terrible sense of uncertainty. Perhaps everything he had planned and everything his grandfather had envisaged was, in the final analysis, a simple dream. Could it ever be possible that through just one single electronic intervention this huge volume of knowledge could be installed in the mind of humanity, or at least in that of today's Triptych System; and indeed so profoundly that it would literally bring about a reversal in its thinking and actions? This wisdom being prepared for transmission represented the results of a process which had lasted for centuries, centuries that had not shown effective results. Instead of following the wisdom of their philosophers and social teachers, people had chosen to turn to greed. Instead of thinking collectively they thought only of their own interests. They had ended up with a logic in the educational system which saw affluence as the only factor leading to happiness for society and the individual. The principles of collectivity and sociability had been abandoned. Truth itself had been abandoned. "In the end, perhaps the collapse of a civilization is not caused by its philosophical base", said Michos, unaware that he was shaking his head. "In theory that is a fact. Anyone can turn on a computer and discover that. What corrupts civilizations is human ambition, dogmatism and the conflicts of interest of those who make up the administration. It is too much money that creates the desire to, come what may, acquire more money. It is finally the utopian striving for the material, for materialistic immortality."

And was it possible for such an enormous failure on the part of mankind, caused by the distortion of values, to be reversed by a technological sleight of hand, a game of despair such as the one he was preparing with his friends? A group of friends that was now working alongside him, persuaded by his assurances, to put anonymity and hunger in second place to the direct danger that he had brought upon them with his grandfather's discovery.

From his training in advertising - a necessary qualification for a travelling salesman for pharmaceutical products – he knew very well that the brain operates as a self-regulating system. This means that through everyday use, mental operation and effort eventually change its natural structure to a considerable degree. Thus, if this natural structure had changed so radically since the time, or rather the times, when the principles and knowledge had been formulated which were loaded into the memory of the elder Michalis' "Cumulative-Monographic, Cerebral Tele-education", their attempt today was utopian and condemned to failure from the outset. It was as if he had gone mad, believing that he had suddenly become not a human being but a god, who could overnight create a new world. That could have had some hope of success if the future was simply the result of a war of ideas. Was what he was now involved in not perhaps a war of ideas but a war of dreams? Would his dreams perhaps end as nightmares for him and his partners? He shook his head again. How significant would it be if he and his partners – and Amsey – never saw the light of day tomorrow? Hope, no matter how small, represented something entirely good. He remembered another quotation, from a great mathematician and philosopher which, like lightning, like a priceless gift, reassured him. The great Albert Einstein had once said "The world is a dangerous place to live; not because of the people who are evil but because of the people who don't do anything about it."

• • •

After the hundreds of texts, dialogues, studies, tragedies, decrees, speeches and international agreements on human rights as the pinnacle of worldwide wisdom prepared by Kamel, Michos saw this extraordinary electronic memory reach its conclusion with one final text. This was an extract from the "Epitaph" speech of Pericles:

"... *Our form of government does not imitate the laws of others. On the contrary, we are rather a model to others. Our form of government is called a democracy because its administration is in the hands, not of a few, but of the many. In the settling of private disputes, everyone has equal rights before the law. Election to public office is made on the basis of ability, not on the basis of membership of a particular class. No man is kept out of public office by the obscurity of his social standing because of poverty, as long as he has the ability to be of service to the state. And not only in our public life are we free and open, but a sense of freedom regulates our day-to-day life with each other. We do not flare up in anger at our neighbor when he does what he likes. And we do not show the kind of silent suspicion that causes pain to others, even though it is not a direct accusation. In our private affairs, then, we are tolerant and avoid causing trouble to one another. But in public affairs, we take great care not to break the laws because of the deep respect we have for them. We give obedience to those in public office and we pay special regard to both those laws that are made for the protection of the oppressed and to all the unwritten laws that we know bring disgrace upon the transgressor when they are broken".*

Before Michos could return to his doubts about the success of their mission, Su Dong appeared and informed them with obvious satisfaction that she was ready to propose the musical element they had earlier agreed to use.

For Michos, however, musical content was not among his immediate priorities. He had another serious worry. He had received no reply to the message, again written in their Navajo code, that he had sent to Amsey. And he was gripped by a chilling premonition.

• • •

Time had passed. A good deal of time, without the burning sensation. "The ancestors are here and are helping me. The ancestors are here and are helping me". Amsey took a deep breath: the first since they had begun torturing her. She did not believe for one minute that it was over. She did believe, however, that it had entered a new phase. She felt them lift her and transfer her to an aircraft. Then, quiet. She sensed that someone was close, studying her every movement. And Amsey remained motionless. She did not want to give her tormentors the satisfaction of an involuntary reaction or facial expression. More minutes passed and she felt them removing the adhesive blindfold. She opened and shut her eyes and saw the face monitoring her. It was not that of a defender. It was a handsome man's face. With clear, pale eyes, a fair beard framing its perfect oval shape, a look full of warmth, one might have said with a keen interest in her fate. A beautiful mouth, whose kiss would be particularly desirable. In short, the last thing she was expecting to see when the blindfold was removed.

His voice was equally attractive. Warm, gentle and calm. "Programmed to persuade," Amsey thought automatically.

"What happened was unfortunate," said the voice. Evidently referring to the torture from the defender's red eye. "I wish we had been able to avoid it." With no response forthcoming, Kasper continued, "The defenders believed that on their own they would get the answers they were looking for. It was their mistake because there is always a way to avoid unpleasantness and get what we want. Without pain. I believe pain is always, but always, unnecessary. I assure you. You will see that I am sincere."

Amsey's expression did not change. She looked without reacting into the pale grey eyes of her unknown and charming opponent who, as he spoke, became ever more persuasive, ever more humane.

"You have to understand that it is absolutely vital for me to know what plans were made by the friend you met on Mytilene," continued Kasper. "From his movements I know that he is preparing something that might have negative consequences for order and security. My job is to see to the maintenance of order and security. I have to report whatever occurs in the region. This security has taken humanity centuries to establish and it cannot now be allowed to be put at risk. Global governance, which was once feared by many nations, has demonstrated that it should not be feared. Now we have harmony, wars have ceased and every citizen leads an untroubled life provided he keeps his mind only on his work. We have at last arrived at a sort of Golden Age, an age of Purification, and we have realised our expectations of a world without war or terrorism. Whoever now persists in criminal ways is neutralized not so much by the employment of force as by a simple adjustment to the brain, through control of the circulation, or even through hypnosis."

"If I detect any wrongdoing on your part, believe me, I will be very lenient. Not only because I respect the loyalty shown to your friend and the strength you have shown throughout your ordeal. Not only for these reasons, but primarily because of your irreproachable history. For the way which, until now, you have served the Triptych System and for the significant role you played in the staging of the official celebrations for its tenth anniversary."

The "man opposite", as Amsey had decided to think of him, clearly had a good knowledge of her background and activities. What the "man opposite" did not apparently know about were her origins. He did not appear to understand how much strength she derived from her bond with the tribe's traditions. A strength whose roots were unknown to him and therefore beyond his comprehension. Still immobilized in her chair, she saw a defender approaching. She had no way of reacting. The chemical in the injection passed automatically from the robot's finger into her vein. Her body did not respond immediately. "It will come in good time," she thought helplessly, as the "man opposite" continued with his seemingly logical advice.

"If you had answered the questions put to you by my assistants" he was saying, "It would not now be necessary for me to subject you to the truth machine. There a person tells everything, even one with your powers of endurance against the painful practices of the defenders. There you have no way of escape. Because the system that I suspect you and your friend are attempting to rebel against is not only just, as I have explained to you. It is also one hundred percent effective. Something you will discover for yourself from the truth machine."

The "truth device" consisted of a hologram that surrounded Amsey's head with such intensity that her field of vision was reduced to an impenetrable fog. Phrases and questions began to stream directly into her thoughts, without her sense of hearing playing any part. Instinctively she understood that answers would be conveyed to her interrogators via processes relating to her mental operation or even via the degree of blood flow to her brain, and not via verbal means.

"How long have you known the person called Michos Diakakis?" was the first question to which she was aware of giving an immediate mental response. She understood that such a form of interrogation made it impossible to circumvent the truth. The "man opposite" was right to call it the "truth device".

Many questions followed, so many she could not remember them all:

"What exactly is Michos planning and what did he ask you to help him with?"

"In what way did you help him?" "Who apart from you is collaborating with him?" "When does he intend to act?" "Where is his base?" The more this continued, the more pleased Amsey felt about the short length of time of her meeting with Michos, or rather the brevity of the briefing she had received, thanks to which there were many gaps in the information he entrusted to her. Gaps which were bound to prompt fresh questions from the "man opposite".

Kasper was less than satisfied with what his device was transmitting to him. The scale of the electronic intervention planned by Michos seemed surreal, utopian. There came a moment when he thought he might be dealing with a fantasist and paranoid not worth wasting his time and attention on. He thought that if the accused was indeed paranoid, the leadership of the T.S. would not be at all satisfied with his work, in sharp contrast with the past. How could anyone believe that they could affect the thought and change the entire mentality of the Triptych System, and in such a short time as conveyed by Amsey's involuntary answers? How could such a thing happen without a powerful and widespread rebellion? Without a prolonged period of time? Without conflict? He decided to remove Amsey from the truth machine and continue the interrogation in open dialogue with her.

The defender on duty removed the restraints immobilizing her and brought her a glass of fresh fruit juice. She gave him an enquiring look. Her first thought was that this was another move with an ulterior motive related to the information they wished to extract from her. "What information?" she wondered. "Whatever they wanted and whatever I had to tell, I have already given them against my will..."

"I want to give you an idea of my own position and your, let's say, specifications," began Kasper in answer to the questions he sensed were occupying Amsey, before she had the opportunity to say anything. It was clear that her experience with the truth device had created a kind of automatic communication between them both.

"In order to convince you that my intentions are good, not only with regard to yourself but also to the society which, I assume, your good friend Michos is attempting to subvert. I am committed to its protection and it is precisely this society which created me, by selecting only the best character traits, biological, intellectual and ethical. I am the guardian of this society, for which the great, ancient philosopher, Plato – your friend will have heard of him – although it doesn't really matter who it was, said that the guardians must excel, that they must not possess more than what is absolutely necessary. That none of them should own a large residence or anything superfluous, but that neither should they want for anything. That they should know they possess gold and silver in their pious hearts so the physical version is not necessary for them. Because physical gold leads to corruption, while theirs is incorruptible and uncontaminated. They are the only ones, of all the citizens, who are not permitted to use or touch gold and silver. If ever these people acquired their own land, houses and money, they would cease to be the allies of the rest and would become enemies and tyrants, living their entire lives hating and being hated by others, abusing and being abused; they would be more afraid of their internal than their external enemies and thus both they and the city would begin to decline... It is a great lesson that power only keeps good and beneficial company with morality."

Amsey was still trying to recover from the distress of the interrogation and the ordeal of the truth device. She did not however hide her interest in what the "man opposite" was saying to her. Instinctively, she wanted to understand just how sincere he was being. Certainly he believed that he was a perfect guardian for the protection of society outside in the real world. Did he believe, however, that this real-life society was as perfect as himself? That his quality of ethics ensured an equivalent social justice in the rest of the world? She decided to find out. Anyway, the tolerable phase of her life was over, so she had nothing to lose by learning something more about how the otherwise interesting man sitting opposite her really thought.

"That your good and beneficial morals sit comfortably with power....is perhaps reasonable. But do your morals and power sit comfortably with justice as it is meted out in the outside world? Do they sit comfortably with the manner in which those confined to the sewers live, and with those who are paid one hundredth of the income of those who occupy powerful positions in the power structure, as you say? How can they sit comfortably alongside the person who works for ten hours in a mine with a defender breathing down his neck in case he should take an unscheduled, even five minute, break? In the final analysis, what is it that you are the faithful and ethical guardian of? With your morals, it would be worth protecting something moral in itself, a moral society. But when the moral guardian protects an immoral society, a society of slaves, what is the point of the guardian being moral?"

"The morals of the guardian are always a basic factor with regard to justice," replied Kasper calmly, "Even if there are injustices and offences in society. The guardian must be there to discover them and correct them. So much the worse if the guardian himself is decadent and corrupt. Then there is no hope of improvement. Even in a just society, a corrupt guardian will lead the society first to a moral and finally to a material catastrophe. On the contrary, if there are injustices as you maintain, an honest guardian can correct many of them."

"He can correct specific wrongdoing. Wrongdoing that stems from personal transgressions, but not however the wrongdoing that constitutes basic flaws in the leadership of society. Like the ones I've just referred to. Finally, your personal position, as you explained with such ease, that is, the ownership of divine gold rather than the physical variety, has no meaning for the poor wretch living like a worm in the ground. For the terrified passerby who does not know when he might receive the burning treatment from the red eye of a defender." Amsey was no longer in the mood to make concessions to the "man opposite".

"Because the society that you protect," she continued, "Has destroyed the middle class, the class, that is, which constitutes the precondition for the existence of any sort of democracy. That has left only two classes, the ruling class and the slaves. It has managed to substantially obliterate the boundaries between nation-states, to impose a single governmental system without the slightest trace of representation for its citizens or rather residents. A system consisting of oligarchies who elect from among themselves those who will serve best, aided by a single armed military or police presence. And just one basic rule: those who obey the law and the global inter- government are rewarded with the means of survival. Those who rebel against the system die of hunger or are a target for whoever wishes them to disappear. That is the society that you are protecting. Without democracy, without equality, without humanity."

"'When a society is not healthy within reasonable limits, democracy can be not only dangerous but catastrophic' another western writer of the last century said'", answered Kasper in what was almost a murmur. As if he had given up the effort to try to put Amsey's thoughts in order. Or as if he did not want the contrast between them to be so obvious. "I only have to remind you of the massacres and upheavals commonplace in the early years of the century. Which spread not only through Asia and Africa but throughout Europe: the outrages committed by religious fanatics, the armed conflicts for oil and water, the instability and danger endured by hundreds of millions. Democracy is not a gift to be given, that the receiver is always ready to appreciate and use for the benefit of his fellow human beings, particularly when extreme political or religious fanaticism holds sway.

Democracy requires some sort of preparation through tradition, a trust in the freedom of all people to choose what they wish to believe. If this preparation does not exist then we end up with the situation we were in before we were forced to construct today's society which, it is true, permits few freedoms but has at least ensured a daily life without unforeseen dangers."

For a few minutes he waited for a response from his prisoner but this never came. He was confident that his words had perhaps produced the desired effect on her mind. He turned and altered the parameters on his "Logic" card, giving instructions for the immediate arrest of Michos and his collaborators. He had however decided against the risk of being seen as paranoid by his superiors. The charge he would make in his report would be of a much less serious nature than suggested by the dialogue with Amsey when using the truth device. Michos would be charged with being a dangerous, paranoid maniac capable of bringing about social disorder. He also decided he must interrogate the lover of the official owning the stolen gold "Logic" card. Klara.

8
SILVERDAY

As always, Hassan was enjoying his working breakfast. He had switched on the holographic transmitter and was following the "Tito and Titi" news, which was preparing viewers for the Persephone mission.

The "Persephone" programme was among other major projects and it was the one that Hassan had undertaken to instil in the public psyche by advertising its expected material benefits. The programme had been formulated by the T.S. when it was noted that the clashes of the mid-century had left a large part of the population, now marginalized and "semi-criminalized", in need of control. Creating more guards and camps proved inadequate and the idea was simultaneously born that the "criminal" population was less of a threat to society than to the political system. The most effective solution was to punish the guilty party immediately he was assessed to be seriously intent on committing a crime, rather than the authorities having to wait for the crime to actually occur. These circumstances required a huge increase in government intervention. Something which subsequently necessitated the use of defenders. But even this innovation did not appear to be enough to control the phenomenon of antisocial behavior and consequent reactions. Then one enterprise remembered the old "Persephone" plan.

Its realization had been indefinitely postponed years before because no volunteers could be found to participate in the risky experiment. The current rebirth of the programme planned to incorporate those potential law-breakers possessing skills useful to the expedition. Simultaneously, the appropriate use of educational hypnotism was now permitted to prepare candidate travelers for the enterprise. Something that would prove far easier if the conditions of their internment were made harsh enough and might last for a lengthy period, perhaps even for life. In the event of there being whole families among the prospective candidate occupants of the "Space Ark"- as some were calling the spacecraft making the Persephone" journey – there had to be some way of minimizing possible adverse reactions to the programme for parents to decide to take their children with them rather than leave them behind on Earth.

Here, the rumour that children left behind might be used as organ donors had helped. It was a rumour which, without being completely baseless, was the reason why Hassan, for the first time in his life, felt uncomfortable. He had always believed making money by whatever means to be the first aim in life, and no means had ever caused him distaste so long as it resulted in the appropriate gain. However, each time, such as right now, that he saw his creations Tito and Titi promoting the Persephone programme, he could not prevent an involuntary palpitation, like a sudden irregularity of the heart-beat, when he thought of the fate awaiting those children left behind by their parents on Earth. Where, according to his own propaganda, the Persephone programme was being planned to save the human race.

• • •

"What are you thinking?" Klara had woken from a deep sleep. A sleep entirely justified by the unbridled erotic release of that night. He wasn't getting any younger but his constitution and use of the latest methods had made his performance in that department such that anyone in their twenties would have envied him. Above all, however, he was especially gentle, something not common among the younger generation, most of them having fallen prey to the inane interests that inundated society in that century. The most popular subjects of interest were, to give some examples, the music of whatever neo-rock band, the trials and tribulations of some actor, the history behind a perfume, and other equally insipid subjects. Others, to impress a woman, subjected their bodies to absurd surgical procedures, from 3D images replacing the original tattoos to aberrations such as prosthetic nipples and testicles. They believed that by so doing they would join a new class of genetically modified aristocrats. Hassan excluded all such ideas from his life early on and kept a combination of enjoyment and tenderness as his only goal in the realm of love-making, which he believed was the main ingredient of happiness. More important even than his desire for profit.

"Hassan?" He turned and stroked her cheek. "Weren't you angry with me?" "Why should I have been angry with you?" "Because of what I told you yesterday when you turned on the hologram…"

"Don't think about it. Perhaps you were right to react like that." He thought for a little. "You must know that you are important to me and that our relationship is my whole life." He stopped, searching for the right words. "I make no secret of having tried for some time now to find a way of having you all to myself. Through somehow compensating your second lover so that he leaves you."

Klara did not react to this unexpected development. "Would you want that?" asked Hassan. He looked into her eyes. Two tears were welling up in them. And a hesitant smile was lighting up her beautiful face. "Are you serious? Would something like that be possible, after everything that Terence has…?"

"I'm serious about wanting it and I can make it happen. Provided you want it too."

The tears and smile suddenly became a flood of light enveloping him and covering him with all the warmth and gratitude that the young woman could express. They held each other in supreme abandonment, above and beyond the erotic fever that normally overwhelmed them, their passion a whirling tornado. As if they were united in a new relationship. More human, more uninhibited and more real, all at the same time. More honest and more profound. It was this happy moment that was interrupted by the heavy knock at the bedroom door.

The two defenders that appeared when the door was opened were similar to all those that Hassan had seen before. Only these seemed very different because they were not concerned with someone else, about whom Hassan would have been indifferent. They were concerned with him and even more so with Klara, as they immediately announced in their strident, metallic voices. They had been ordered to arrest Klara, they said, for a serious breach of the law. And to inform Hassan that he would henceforth be under surveillance for a related offence. Klara, given only a few moments to dress, turned to Hassan, frightened and pale as she left the room. To try to assure him that she had no idea what they could be accusing her of. Despite not knowing, she felt that, from one moment to the next, her charmed life replete with all the luxury one could possibly desire had collapsed and vanished. From now on she was nothing.

Hassan, now on his feet, half-dressed and speechless, knew that any attempt to argue with the defenders would be useless. They were not programmed to be convinced; they were only programmed to faithfully follow orders.

"Who instigated this order?" he wondered, "and what breach of the law is Klara accused of?"

He went to the large window and was just in time to see the defenders escorting Klara into the air-car. He thought that this might be the last time he would ever see her and felt again that involuntary palpitation in his heart. Just as when he had thought about the fate of the children destined to be organ donors.

He must find an explanation. He picked up his "Logic" card and tried to communicate with colleagues and friends who he knew had some influence, but without success. As if his card had been completely blocked. He did finally manage to find a member of Political Security who undertook to find out. The response he received a few minutes later increased the shock he was in. He sat down with his head in his hands. For the first time in his life he was without something or someone that he cared about. Klara had been accused, the member of the security service told him, of aiding Amsey in the theft of his "Logic" card, his gold "Logic" card.

Tito's hologram was so close it was almost touching him as it began to demonstrate his latest idea. The idea that was beginning to make Hassan prouder even than the "Persephone" project. Here one could be certain of a plethora of applications, perhaps not useful right away in everyday life, but which, Hassan was certain, with the correct holographic promotion would in a few months evolve into a valuable asset with huge returns, together with his own increased social and economic advancement. But for the first time he noticed that personal success no longer held the priority that had gnawed at him all his life. He made a movement as if to push the "Tito" hologram away and left the lavish room where he had experienced the unprecedented feeling that night. The feeling that he had a new priority within him, a higher meaning. More humane than glory, more desirable even than money.

• • •

Su Dong made a sudden, dramatic appearance while Babar and his friends were adding the final details to their master plan.

"I have the answer!" she exclaimed, controlling her enthusiasm with difficulty.

The men turned their heads in unison. "What answer?"

"The musical element of our message. Music that has to be pleasant but dynamic, that can be conveyed harmoniously along with the ideas we wish to transmit, that will be immediately recognizable and set a tone of authenticity and optimism."

Michos gave an involuntary yawn. He had often wondered at women's patience. He did not want to upset Babar, however. "You have three minutes to explain. Your answer, I mean," he confined himself to saying.

"It is called 'Joy'", said Su Dong, grasping her opportunity. "It is a piece composed by Bach."

"The 'Ode to Joy' by Beethoven", Michos corrected her.

"No. Simply 'Joy'," repeated Su Dong. "It is often confused with Beethoven's composition and, yes, it is very similar, but it is not the same. It is 'Joy' by Bach and I will let you hear it right now."

Music was instantly heard as Su Dong explained the powerful cognitive and aesthetic messages suddenly filling the little shack.

"Notice," she began. "The music begins with four chimes, as if calling us all to attention, and continues with the tentative repetition of a motif, as if awaiting our full attention for what is to follow...And then comes an intense release of sounds that powerfully mark a birth of optimism. There follows magnificent exhilaration and a persistent countering of dissonance; like a repeated promise to mankind of gaining permanent happiness if it perseveres in the principles being proclaimed. It repeats, I would say, the promise of well-being and confirms that now everything will change. It ends with an insistent coda of anticipation and certainty, I believe, that we will respond to this universal call. With the monumental cry: Let us go forward together!"

A hesitant silence followed Su's interpretation. "It is quite possible," she added, "that it will tie in with the principles we are trying to implant in the minds and consciences of people. They will hear the music and see in their imaginations the principles that an individual, and above all a leader, needs. They will apply these principles and listen to the music of Joy."

Su Dong stopped, unaware that her arms were still raised high in explanation. Her face shone with emotion.

"Three minutes." Her voice did not hide her enthusiasm. "That's the figure you gave me and that's what may change the fortunes of our endeavour. It is music that is listened to with pleasure, it is dynamic, harmonises with the ideas of freedom, optimism and hope we wish to convey, is immediately recognizable and provides an element of finesse, honesty and sincerity."

Michos looked at Babar. He shrugged his shoulders and opened his arms as if to say, "What have we got to lose?"

"Let's go on," decided Michos. "Add Su's music, and you, Kamel, finish up the texts. I have the impression there is very little time left. I'm receiving no messages from the collaborator who has been such a help to me. I fear she may have been taken. Let's assume that we may have only tonight."

"If they have got her," Babar added, "the System's interrogation methods are now extremely effective and produce results faster than ever before. What I'm saying is that the only thing the System will not know about is what the detainee herself doesn't know. If she knows a lot, that is what the System will now know too. And this regardless of the most heroic defence," he added, to avoid Michos misinterpreting his remarks.

"There was a lot she didn't know. But I still believe that we don't have much time," replied Michos and he glanced at what Kamel was doing at that moment. He was now busy with the political knowledge and influence of the east. He had added whole screeds from the sayings of Confucius as well as those elements of his teachings which could be combined with similar elements from Socrates.

The situation brought to Michos's mind all he had been informed at an holographic conference he had attended recently : namely that both Socrates and Confucius considered ethics to be the basis of politics and believed that the crises of a State were caused by ethical shortcomings. Since therefore the two philosophies aim at the formulation of the "remedy" needed to save society from chaos, the texts demand priority is given to the study of a so- called universal ethic. For this reason, dialogue, and indeed constructive and serious dialogue between ancient cultures and their modern equivalents, is more necessary than ever before. And here begins one of the many points which, by their very differences, constitute unifying links between cultures. In order for it to become reality at the cultural level and not simply at the individual level, as exists in Confucian theory. Since Chinese thinkers of all persuasions never aimed at leaving things unchanged in their substance. On the contrary, they considered these shifts as the only stability in the world. From this thinking came the fundamental Confucian notion that a person exists only from the moment that she or he enters into a relationship with another.

The conclusion of the conference was that only close relations between two cultures are capable of accomplishing the feat: To show, that is, that they "exist" because they collaborate and for that reason are "productive". That they produce the rules of the collective ethic needed for Purification. Not of course on the terms laid down by the T.S., but through common rules, common values, common models and commonly accepted forms of behavior. This effort is not easy. Whoever undertakes it must know that they have undertaken to realise a huge feat. It will be difficult. It will take much time. It will be a life's work. It will however be the supreme work of culture which will contribute to human happiness and world peace.

"If the security system hasn't got all the information, if your collaborator hasn't told them everything, then there is a chance they'll arrive a lot sooner than if she had confessed everything", said Babar suddenly, as if struck by an idea – an unpleasant one this time.

Michos looked at him anxiously.

"Having definitely decided to find you, the T.S. will activate their individual-tracking system. They don't often do so because it demands the complex and expensive combined working of electronic systems. But I believe they'll do it in our case. The suppression tables at the information centre, in your case at least – you having come into direct contact with your collaborator – will have reclassified you from orange to red. In a few minutes from now I estimate that the defenders will have got to us."

The ensuing half hour was more like bedlam than organized work. Each one tried to wind up his work in the best way that time allowed. The data on the whole electronic "flash" was locked. Babar's holographic computer was programmed and transmission of the material was completed in the final ten minutes. Babar crouched down in the centre of the room and lifted the rug to reveal a trap-door. He opened it and to the sound of the lapping waters of the great lake.

"We have a boat. It's old-technology and slow but I think it gives us some hope of escape. We have to go down a rope ladder," he said, hugging the holographic computer close to him.

A small boat was moored directly under the shack. They all managed to somehow fit in and then Su started up the engine. As they left the cover of the jetty, lights appeared in the distance approaching fast. The defenders were close.

"We have to separate," said Babar. "If we don't, they're going to catch us all. If we separate, some of us at least stand a chance of getting away."

"What should we do?" asked Michos.

"We'll drop you and Kamel off on the shore near here. From there Kamel can get to the camp where his wife and children are. He may be able to hide there. For you," he said to Michos, "I believe there is only one place where there is any hope of them not finding you immediately. I'll show you how to get to the eagle-hunters. They are a primitive group that have never adapted to the present and yet are ignored by the System. They are untouched by anything new and live in remote areas. I'll explain how you can get the local air-car. But be prepared for extreme cold in the place where you find them."

Michos nodded his agreement. "And you?"

"We'll go on to the opposite shoreline. We'll try to stay hidden in an area we know. Just until we find a way to slip back into Su's homeland. I'm hoping they'll have forgotten her misdemeanor over the dowry." Babar was sure to be smiling in the darkness, despite this being the most desperate moment of his life.

"Do you think our message went out alright?" asked Michos.

"I'm positive. Your grandfather's system was infallible. As infallible as my Holograph." He looked fondly at the appliance held carefully between his legs. The small waves made the boat's movement erratic and the appliance was his whole life.

"I want to ask you something before I thank you for everything you've done until now. You, Kamel and Su," said Michos. "If we have achieved our goal, the satisfaction for each of us will, I think, be enough. Thank yous will not be necessary. But if we have failed, I still want to thank you for helping in spite of the dangers involved. Before, we were only waiting for the danger, but now it's almost on top of us, and it's deadly."

"We chose to do what we did." Kamel had not spoken until now. His mind was far away, with his family. He lifted his eyes.

"I believe," he said, looking at Michos, "that my thanks are at least owed to you. That you chose me to help you in this task. Or rather in this endeavour. We don't know how it will end..."

"Let's hope that everything goes well and that some things in our lives will change, so that when we meet again we'll be able to speak without fear and without the pressures of time." Michos had in mind what he had begun to say earlier to Babar. "I want to ask you for something that you may find difficult to accept." Babar gave him a questioning look. "I want you to respect my grandfather's wishes," continued Michos. "If his discovery were to fall into the wrong hands, it would be better if it were lost altogether. It could cause an even worse situation than the one we have today. Even complete catastrophe."

"Do you want me to throw the whole programme into the water?" Babar was unprepared for that.

"If you are right and our signal and its contents have reached their destination. If it has already arrived and is producing the results hoped for, then it is no longer needed", replied Michos. "Again, if we have failed and they capture us with it, it will be used to impose an even more cruel slavery. Slavery no longer the result of violent power but slavery of the mind and spirit. That's why I believe the only honest solution we have right now is to destroy everything we have tried to create over the last few days."

The half-darkness was not enough to hide from Babar the desperation reflected in Michos' eyes. Babar pushed his thoughts aside. In any case the shoreline where he would leave his two passengers was now quite close. He bent down, removed the mnemonema from the computer, wrapped them carefully together with a weight attached and looked back at Michos waiting expectantly.

"I understand your sadness and your reluctance, my friend, but you have to do it," murmured Michos.

With a single movement, Babar catapulted the package out of the boat. Into the black waves. He let out a long sigh. "I just hope we don't regret it, that we won't need it again," he said quietly and directed his attention to finding a spot where he reckoned they could tie up.

• • •

9
CORALDAY

"Just a moment to get my breath back". The sight of the silvery lake stretching out before him in the first light of dawn saw off his breathlessness. It was a spellbinding sight and he wondered why so many poets were inspired by the sight of the sea or a lake, yet employed only the colours of sunset. Why were there not just as many poets singing the praises of the dawn colours. Kamel, gazing at the vast mirror of water before him, was so enthralled that for a moment he forgot the problem occupying him: what would happen to his family? What would be their fate following the help he had given to the unknown Greek who persuaded him that the spirit is stronger than brute force, that a dream is more effective than reality. That one technology is capable of completely dominating another.

"And why not?" he said aloud to the surrounding wilderness. "There can be hope even when that possibility is very small," he then thought, and he straightened up for the walk to the Purification Camp. After all, the fate of the camp's in-mates could not get worse than it already was. A mission into space without the hope of coming back. Coming back from where? Perhaps from Hell. That was why the manned mission to Mars was named "Persephone". His knowledge of ancient mythology made him suddenly aware of the project's prospects, as well as why it had been given that name. The daughter of the goddess Demeter, Persephone, was kidnapped by Hades who wished to make her his wife. Her mother, however, abandoned her work – to make agriculture, particularly cereals flourish– to dedicate all her time to looking for her daughter. The danger of famine over the entire Earth made Zeus intervene and Hades agreed to set Persephone free. But Zeus laid down one condition: that Persephone should not take any sort of nourishment while in the Underworld. Persephone, however, could not resist the seeds of a sweet pomegranate offered by Hades. And Zeus, as was natural since he was the father of the Gods, discovered the deception and condemned Persephone to spend four months of each year in Hades and only the remaining months on Earth. So, for those four months the Earth dries, becomes cold and almost dies. "As those being readied by the T.S. for the journey into space will finish up," Kamel ended with the dark thought...

He sat a few more minutes, marveling at the infinity of the lake now beginning to brighten its silver appearance with tints of blue. He sighed deeply and continued on his way to the Camp.

At some point an air-car passed over him heading north and he guessed it was of the type that the T.S. would have dispatched to search for him. However, he remembered that the night when they were putting their programme together, Babar had ensured the hours were multiplied and loaded onto each member of the team's "Logic" card. The cards would indicate that they were still at the fisherman's shack for many hours to come. This gave them some hope of remaining free for a little longer.

• • •

Nora and the two boys had just returned to ground-level when Kamel arrived at the Camp. They showed him the enormous dome covering the centre of an open square. Nora explained that beneath the dome was the entrance to a shaft that led deep underground to installations that simulated life on Mars and the structures that the manned mission would be putting together for the first settlers to live and work in.

"They are small three-storied chambers containing all the bare essentials for life and the food production necessary for the survival of the first travellers to the Dream Planet," said Nora to Kamel. The serenity with which she described how they were led into the lift, the depth to which they were taken, how perfect the installations down there were, alerted Kamel to a certain composure in her face that he was at a loss to explain. He made no comment. He turned to his sons. Marios, eight years old and Alexandros, five, studied him with intense interest, as if he had been gone for far longer than was actually the case. He asked them what they thought of all they had seen on the brief trip underground and Marios was eager to tell him. He described the circular houses with beds on one floor, the cultivation of crops on another, and the third floor with living quarters, a kitchen and everything the travelers would need. When Kamel asked if they were worried about embarking on such a long journey, Marios replied that it was not so long ago that even the Earth where we live was considered a part of the extra-terrestrial universe.

Here Nora interrupted the conversation by making a sign to Kamel not to question the children further.

"Everything we saw there gave us more courage than you can imagine," she said. "It made us feel more physically and psychologically responsible and bolstered our confidence. I feel refreshed and I think that the children, too, can't wait for the big day to come. It will be an amazing experience..."

"And I saw, too, how beautiful the place we are going to is," piped up little Alexandros.

"How did you do that?" Kamel was unable to hide his intense anxiety over the changes he could see had occurred in the minds of his loved ones within the space of just a few hours.

"It was in my dream." "Not only in the dream," cut in Marios. "It really is a Heavenly State, much more beautiful than the one we know in Alexandria."

"Leave your father. He is tired. He was walking all night and he must rest a little."

Kamel shook his head. He could not believe what he had heard. He thought for a moment and then asked:

"Where can I find Vlado? To get more information about this journey."

• • •

"Remember the 'God helmet'?" Vlado asked Kamel. Stunned by the sudden and irrational transformation in Nora and the children, Kamel had come to Vlado to get answers to his questions. His first impression was that Vlado seemed not to have been affected in the same way as Kamel's family. Listening to Kamel's questions, Vlado nodded his understanding. He then asked:

"Remember the 'God Helmet'?" Kamel shook his head.

"What is it?"

"Many years ago, serious experiments began on soldiers in the army of the great power of the time, in an effort to eliminate the effects of traumatic incidents experienced during the wars that had then devastated various parts of the world. Appliances passed ultra-sound waves through the brain for the purpose of reducing unpleasant emotions and memories. However, they also created a new mental and spiritual situation, by increasing the brain's capacity to react in extreme situations and diminishing to a great extent the subject's emotional world. Their purpose was to achieve the complete eradication of fear and empathy. Those are the two emotions that must be absent for the creation of the 'perfect soldier'. In the early days, this was achieved using a helmet filled with electrodes and known as the 'God Helmet'. However, many years have passed since then and the technology is now far advanced. Today, the same effects can be achieved using far more discreet means."

"Such as?" "Such as congregating people somewhere and exposing them to energy from electromagnetic fields. The subjects feel very little, something like an invisible breeze, but the outcome is guaranteed. The brain is bombarded by high-powered radio waves with dramatic results. Which is why the initial helmet was called the 'God helmet'. A person undergoing such 'therapy' feels that he has been cured by a divine hand, as if he has seen God himself."

"When does this so-called 'therapy' take place?"

"During sleep. The electronic features are now so sophisticated that the procedure is undetectable to anyone lacking special training. They are implanted into everyday items."

"What did you do to avoid this 'therapy'?"

"They don't want me to be - how can I put this delicately? - emotionally and spiritually modified. They don't want me in a state of virtual reality. We know that all thought, feeling and behaviour is regulated by the brain. They need me to work the transition system for the duration of the voyage. That's why I've been left emotionally and spiritually intact."

"Tell me what I can do to save my family," Kamel could not restrain his anguish.

"I don't think you can do anything," replied Vlado. "Think logically. If the journey finally takes place and your wife and children are among those selected, these preparations will help them survive and not suffer from the terrible distress they would otherwise experience. The planet represents a new way of life for them, a place of flowers and brilliance. With fabulous landscapes that promise pleasures wonderful not only to the eyes but for the other senses too. Images of a paradise that does not exist in real life. A heavenly place, as your young son described it to you. If on the other hand they are not selected, then I only hope that the consequences of their 'therapy' as we call it will be temporary. Because, you see, there are other methods, more permanent ones, which fortunately have not been used."

In response to Kamel's questioning look, Vlado added: "Alterations to brain function have now advanced to the point where these can be implemented – particularly in the case of serial law-breakers, but also others labelled "undesirables" by the System – through radical DNA restructuring. With the aid of nanotechnology, implantation can occur via food in-take, clothing or even via injections of nanocomposites which permanently re-channel the brain in the direction desired by the System. And with no possibility of a return to the subject's original state. Fortunately for everyone at the Camp, the System has chosen not to use this method in preparations for the great journey."

Vlado did not add one other thing he still had on his mind. Giving the complete picture is often not only undesirable but dangerous. The information he had received from his sources was worrying, to put it mildly, but he saw no reason for enlightening Kamel at this moment.

• • •

Pressed far back into his seat, Michos wondered how much longer this vertical climb into the skies would continue. Because the journey he had just begun really was an upward climb through the air. The automated air-car, in order to arrive at the required altitude for Michos' stipulated destination, was manoeuvring more like an aeroplane taking off than a land vehicle. From the small window, he could see the snow-covered slopes of the Altai close alongside the vehicle as it shot by, leaving in its wake dazzling flurries of ancient, crystallized white snow. The vehicle was carrying him to the territory of the hunters, an area that according to Babar had been left unchanged by the invasion of the Triptych System, in an environment still dominated by hunting, golden eagles and fur. And besides, Babar had added certain interesting snippets of information to the above. Because it was said that eagle hunters guided the eagles with their thoughts, Chinese researchers at the Centre for Robotic Engineering in Sandong had some years ago used members of their tribe in experiments researching tele-navigation by pigeons. In the experiments, electrodes stimulated parts of the birds' brains enabling them to receive "instructions" about which routes they were to take.

However, as Babar went on to say, efforts were soon abandoned when it was discovered that the eagle hunters did not rely on implanted electrodes for their work. Being the survivors of an ancient tribe that had played an important role in antiquity as local go-betweens guiding travelers along the "Silk Road", they employed methods that exploited their natural gift for extra-sensory perception. A perception common among those alive at the dawn of humanity but lost many centuries ago. Indeed, Babar joked that the eagle hunters, in order to deter the Chinese scientists, claimed that their success in the field of tele-navigation of hawks and golden eagles was the result of owners spreading spittle on the heads of their birds, and that this facilitated the transference of thoughts from hunter to bird.

When he was travelling to Babar's shack, Michos had had the opportunity to meet some of these hunters - quaint survivors of a remote and forgotten culture. So he now set off hoping that in the inaccessible environment where the hunters lived, it would perhaps be difficult for the defenders to track him down. However, from the moment he set out, he was beset by doubts over the wisdom of his decision. His reasoning had less to do with the effectiveness of this move than with the regret he felt at involving yet another group of people in his bizarre scheme; people who did not have or want to have any association with science or technology. It was a doubt akin to the way he felt when he got Alison or Amsey involved in his plan. However, there was one great difference with today's move. Amsey had made a conscious decision to help him and her help had proved crucial to the success of his plan.

"Success?" he wondered. "Who has told me that we have succesfuly achieved the result we wanted?"

At some point the air-car ceased its ascent and began to travel horizontally. It was clear it had reached the altitude of the hunters' territory. "Altitude: 2354 metres", he read on the information display of the vehicle's control panel in front of him.

Small cabins scattered across the snow-covered ground confronted him when he eventually emerged from the air-car. The robot pilot gave a sign that he was leaving. The cold was penetrating and Michos glanced quickly around him. At that moment several people emerged from a cabin and he walked towards them. He had prepared an excuse for his arrival, a pretext however that he knew would not be very convincing. He saluted them and, hoping that Russian was a language that these people so isolated from the rest of world still understood, uttered a few words of greeting. The hunters showed him to the entrance of the first cabin and, entering together, they sat around a fire in the centre. The shadows around him moved constantly and randomly, increasing the dizziness that had plagued him throughout the night to an intolerable level. But he managed to find the courage to explain that he was a pharmaceuticals supplier and that the purpose of his visit was to ascertain which medicines were needed by the inhabitants of the settlement. Showing no reaction, the hunters offered him tea. It was the most satisfying Michos had ever tasted. Its warmth entered his frozen body and its slightly greasy taste went almost unnoticed.

• • •

"You did what you could", he heard, which seemed odd since there was no one else in the cabin. He knew that he had also fallen into a deep sleep as soon as the hunters had brought him in there. His eyes remained closed without his being aware of whether he was actually sleeping or not. A long pause followed before he heard once again the voice resonating throughout his consciousness. "Certainly you did whatever was possible."

"Who is this?" Michos wondered, but his thought was immediately understood.

"I am the Elder of Baidou..." Despite his efforts, Michos could not open his eyes. He could not wake up.

"Where do I know you from?" Michos tried to find some sense in the mist of extreme anxiety enveloping him. "What is happening?" he was thinking.

"I speak to you, and you answer. That is what is happening."

"He can hear my every thought!" he thought again.

"You are hearing my thought, not my voice."

"Who are you?"

"You do not know me. I know you."

"From where?" Michos continued the incredible conversation.

"From your good intentions towards your fellow human beings. I must..."

Michos did not hear the rest of the sentence because of the creaking cabin door as an eagle hunter entered. He shook Michos' arm.

"They are coming to take you," he said breathlessly in Russian. As he came out of the cabin he saw in the daylight two shiny objects approaching from the sky.

"I've just been hearing a voice. As if an old man was speaking to me..."

The eagle hunter who had awoken him looked at him with renewed interest.

"Come and be introduced to him," he said. "He's in this next cabin."

He was an amazing figure. The old man could not have had a more elderly appearance, his long, narrow face framed by a wild forest of a beard, eyes that shone yet remained motionless, as if they had long ago acquired the lustre of eternal wisdom. As if there was nothing they had not seen. An open hand was extended towards Michos.

He turned to the eagle hunter and gave him a questioning look. He was not sure whether the motionless body before him was alive or not.

"I am," the quiet voice from inside him replied unexpectedly. "I am still in this world." The expression of the eyes had not changed. The face remained the same. The hand had not moved.

"You did whatever you could," Michos heard the voice again.

"I don't know what I achieved,"Michos just had time to wonder, as the door burst open and a defender appeared.

"You did what you could," he heard again the voice inside him, as he felt his earlobe burning from the flash of the defender's third eye.

10
GOLDDAY

The journey only lasted an hour. Hassan Porter, however, was not to be satisfied. He had wasted a whole day looking for someone high up in the system, someone to help him find Klara. When he saw that all his trouble had been in vain, he decided to go to the security section for the Middle East and Eastern Mediterranean.

He took the fastest air-car available and was now looking at the fine edifice before him, the Tripartite Committee of Inspectors for the Eastern Mediterranean. It had been erected on top of the Second Dam, in the Mediterranean; second in size only to the dam of Gibraltar, it connected the coast of Sicily with the small island of Pantelleria and the coast of Africa. The area was given the name Kosyra by its first, Greek inhabitants. Later it had become known by its Arabic – and far more poetic - name of "The Daughter of the Winds". The building was circular in shape. Reminiscent from above of those electric light switches widespread in the twentieth century, but its dimensions were far greater than those of the Library of Alexandria, which its architects had clearly taken as their model. To right and left he could just make out the two ends of the Second Dam that linked Europe with Africa.

At the entrance to the building, Hassan gave his particulars and asked to see the person in charge of Mediterranean Security. The two robots who dealt with his request said nothing but indicated a seat where he could wait. After a short time, they showed him to an express lift and then to an office where he was received by another robot, this one bearing insignia of higher rank.

"I asked to see the person responsible for security in the region," he calmly protested. It was impossible for him to say precisely what he meant, which was that he wanted to see a human and not a robot, because such a request in itself would have been considered something akin to racism and have provoked a negative reaction.

"He is busy at present," came the metallic, nasal response from the mechanized official behind the desk. "I am authorised to assist you. What can I do for you?"

"I have a friend," explained Hassan, and went on to describe the manner in which the defenders had arrested Klara and his fruitless efforts since the previous day to find out where she was being held and what had happened to her. He did not omit to mention his position in the T.S., the services he was responsible for and those he had performed.

The advantage of the defenders, and generally all robotic appliances, thought Hassan, was that they were not obliged to express their thoughts. Not possessing feelings, they were able to receive the best or the worst piece of news, to perform acts of a pleasant or highly unpleasant nature, without one being able to discern the slightest change in their demeanor. All this over and above the fact that as machines they guaranteed their leaders absolute discipline and obedience without any human hesitation. The robot official before him busied itself briefly with its "Logic" card and then turned to Hassan.

"I know where she is," the nasal, metallic voice sounded pleasant to Hassan. This time.

"Where is she? May I visit her?"

"She is in a wing of the building. But I have to tell you that the news is not good," the voice answered.

"Not good? What do you mean?"

"She has died of heart failure."

"That's not possible. I'm not hearing right. It can't be her. She's still so young. She's mine. She's only mine. We had an agreement. I didn't hear properly. It isn't her." His thoughts came all at once and he did not know which one he wanted to shout out first.

"It isn't her. What do you mean, heart failure? Why?"

"The medical report states she had some sort of cardiac weakness."

"That's impossible. Look at your papers again. Type her name in again. Please. It's a mistake, it's the wrong person."

"My assistants can accompany you to see her if you wish." It was as if the voice now contained an unnecessary note of coldness, although this was not possible. Hassan put his hands to his head, he felt he was about to explode. His eyes had filled with tears, he was hardly breathing and his heart was pounding. He turned and with difficulty followed the two defenders who had brought him to the office.

• • •

His eyes fixed on the door of the crematorium, Hassan was struggling to make time pass without losing his mind. "What have I spent my life doing?" he wondered. "What have I done to deserve something like this? Since childhood I've tried, thanks to my father's advice, to adapt myself to the demands of the system. I renounced Islam, my religion. I grew up an exemplary follower of the new neutral religion. I was a leading light in every move aimed at the predominance of the Triptych System. I followed the directives of the official line, of the 'California Ideology'. I helped to set up, with no resistance, the economy now revealed to be an economy of low wages and enforced labour. I encouraged the creation of a world of profound inequalities, intense exploitation of labour and prolonged hardship for everyone. I promoted the positive presentation of suppression, poverty, exploitation and hunger. I helped in the creation of a life that some leader at the beginning of the century described with the words: 'Show life in California to be rosy, but life in the rest of the world to stink like the manure that roses need to grow and blossom.'

Why did I give so much assistance to the creative catastrophe that brought about the technology economy? I applied all my knowledge to protect the System from any threat, whether human or electronic, in order for it to continue being forever unjust and inhuman."

"Why?" The question burned in his mind like lava inside a volcano. He wondered how he was still capable of even thinking about it.

The door opened and a defender gestured to him that he could now enter. The lump in his throat choking him had become a mountain. His sight was blurred by the damp darkness that enveloped them as they approached the plastic casket. He put his hand to his mouth as if wanting to stifle a cry. Klara, more beautiful than ever, lay there in what appeared to be a thin, semi-transparent night-dress. For a moment he did not react. He simply thought, "Why did they take her from me? After all I've done for them....They've taken from me the only psychological consolation I had left. For myself. The only source of freedom from my remorse."

On the side of the casket was a label. Klara's name and the cause of death. "Heart failure. Death instantaneous."

Was she perhaps given a bioelectrograph?" he heard himself asking the defender beside him. The rules indeed required that, in a case of unexpected death, the body should undergo bioelectrography which would register certain final reactions of the deceased even for some seconds after the heart had ceased to function. The technique was based on an earlier Russian invention which created an image in blue of the life power as it gradually abandoned the body.

"If it has not yet been done, I would like it to be carried out," he added. "I will personally cover all the expenses involved."

There followed a moment's hesitation before the defender replied that it would ask for instructions. The instructions that came back were positive and a defender immediately appeared holding a bioelectrographic camera.

• • •

"What made me ask for it?" he wondered as he felt the blood rising threateningly to his head. His vision blurred dramatically as he saw the dark blue outline of Klara's torso rise and then vapourise as the life force exited her body. He had seen other such holograms before but none until now that depicted life leaving someone so close to him. Before the shadow showing the final energy, or soul as it was once referred to in bioelectrography, disappeared, Hassan thought he was going to lose his mind. Because the uppermost part of the blue shadow, where his beloved's head had been until the day before yesterday, turned in his direction. Like an infinitesimally brief moment of dark lightning. He might have added that her eyes looked at him as if pleading for something. He felt his reason slipping precariously and shook his head violently, as if he could shake off the wave of insanity overwhelming him. "Do not think!" "Do not think!" he screamed to himself as he rushed from the crematorium.

"And yet she was looking at me, asking me, begging me. What could she have been asking for as a last favour from her lover, a young woman so full of life until yesterday, what was her complaint?" What else other than bitterness that her life was suddenly taken, and she altogether blameless ....The question weighed on Hassan's conscience, as heavily as if his beloved herself had expressed it, in a clear voice, as if more than simply light was projected towards him by the shadow released as her body's final act.

Exiting the chamber, he was confronted by yet another defender asking him to follow. Hassan was led to a small office where he was received by an official. This was the first human being he had met since entering the vast building atop the Second Dam.

"I have an order here, to convey to you the esteem of the Controller of Eastern Europe and the Middle East for your valuable contribution until now in the service of the Triptych System," were the words with which the official received him. "He has asked me to thank you for your contribution and requested that you hand over to me your gold card, it having fallen – without of course you being responsible – into the hands of a stranger. I will replace it with an ordinary card." As he said this, the official placed an ordinary "Logic" card on his desk.

"I will allow you a few minutes to transfer your personal data to the new card before you hand the gold one over to me. Remember, only your personal data."

Thus Hassan Porter found himself alone in a small office inside the Second Dam building, trying to organise his thoughts on the terrible turn of events experienced over the last hours.

"Perhaps even fewer hours remain to me." The thought came to him spontaneously.

• • •

"I have no wish to ignore the significance of morality with regard to questions of technological progress," said Kastor, the head of Security for Central Asia. "Such as nanotechnology and robotics, although today it is difficult to define morality. Because the substance of the issues relating to it has changed radically since the time when life was an unbroken continuation of the primitive picture that prevailed up until the present age of techno-genetics. I wish however to stress the point relating to order and our purpose. We were created to secure order and the security of citizens, and the emergence of artificial, super-natural beings today may endanger our entire society. The field of morality does not belong within our jurisdiction, as it once did when a technological breakthrough occurred in earlier times. When, for example, genetic engineering was first practised, of which all of us holding this discussion are the result. Among the problems was: who has the right to choose this technology for his children, and who does not have that right? How will one who has acquired additional capabilities regard passing these on to his children, and how will a parent lacking these same opportunities for his children react. There are also significant social problems such as their place in society, whether they will be equal to other citizens, whether they will have the same rights to reproduce. Whether it is appropriate for genetics to be used on embryos. All these questions were dealt with at the time. Now, however, we are faced by a future in which a sort of genetically advanced superman might one day be developed, without the protective specifications that existed for our generation to avoid unexpected outcomes for security. For the field of security, that is, to which we have been assigned and for which we are responsible. Who can guarantee however that the greater capabilities we have today will not be outsmarted by some sort of superhuman robot created by a 'biotechnological accident'?"

The Security Officer for Central Asia, Kastor, continued the main theme of his introduction, the effort that must be made by the class of Security Officers to bring an end to experiments aimed at the creation of a robotic superman. Or at least for effective measures to be put in place to control activities that might put the security of society at risk.

At the top of the vast Second Dam building, the officer for the Security of Eastern Europe and the Middle East, Kasper, was following on his hologram the progress of the important teleconference. From his office, beyond the telescopic glass panels forming a 360 degree panorama one could see, with the appropriate adjustments, what was occurring from the shores of Palestine to Gibraltar and from North Africa to the Adriatic. An Adriatic now of course much reduced in size, the sea level having dropped in the Eastern Mediterranean by tens of metres since the Second Dam came into operation. In any case, technological progress had brought about enormous changes in the concept of distance, Kasper thought, demonstrated by this holographic teleconference for a team of security officers from various parts of the world. The special feature of the conference was that all participants had the same origins as Kasper. "Eugenicists" had begun experiments around the middle of the previous century but had intensified their work over the past fifty years. They wished to produce mutated humans with natural or artificial genes, who would become a new class of genetically prepared security officers. The aim was to give the officers not only know-how but also endurance and resistance against any attempts at coercion or terror that a normal person would be unable to withstand. Experiments continued until the eugenicists believed they had achieved the desired optimum results. These were arrived at using two methods: so-called negative and positive human genetic engineering. The first, negative, method aimed at the reversal or removal of genes from cells to inhibit and treat genetic human flaws. The positive method aimed at improving a human and his progeny by increasing performance to an extent that once would have been condemned as genetic doping.

Moral dilemmas did not obstruct efforts until it was considered that a "quality" of the sought for perfect human-being functionary had been achieved. The work was classified in alphabetical order. Series "A", series "B", and so on. Each unsatisfactory series was rejected, creating its own moral problems, but experiments continued until the scientists achieved complete success with Series "K". Kasper and his colleagues belonged to this Series. All those, that is, participating in that day's holographic teleconference. Those present, in holographic form, were the security officer of Western Europe, Katon, of Central Asia, Kastor, of America, Karter, of Australia, Kassios and of Asia, Karlos.

The teleconference had a specific aim. The examination of the possible dangers that might arise from continuing research into eugenics, not only for other people but also for the aims that had led to the creation of the "K" class. The eugenicists were indeed trying to create a type of super-human robot, starting from scratch and using a combination of genetic and neural engineering. The result was potentially extremely dangerous since the eugenicists insisted on experimenting without the required electronic subthreshold stimuli as before. In other words, the necessary protection against any wish to question authority. Kasper and his colleagues believed that this attempt to create a superhuman robot without the necessary safeguards could be highly dangerous for humanity. Of course, the scientists tried to direct their neural engineering to influence the human brain to act for the common good. However, the power technically conferred on these human-robots could not simultaneously rule out an unexpected result, given the complexity in the function of neurons. This excluded the implementation of automated behavior in the desired direction. The "K" functionaries, however, strengthened by their additional intellectual capabilities were more able than other, more natural people, to appreciate the dangers of the neural engineering experiments, without the necessary prior implants and other protective measures.

"What brings about the collapse of a civilization," Kasper had read somewhere, "is not its philosophical foundations, but the ambitions, dogmatism and corruption of the people who make up its administrative structures." And given that ordinary people can destroy a civilization with their weaknesses, imagine what super-human robots might do if not constrained by the necessary components of genetic control...."

• • •

"If no advance provision is made for the necessary components of genetic control," Kasper's thought continued, "then certain constraints must be placed on the actions of the super-humans being produced." He therefore decided to put the main emphasis of the introduction he was preparing for his contribution to the holographic teleconference on the actions of genetic superhumans and little emphasis on their special features since, as things stood, there was not time enough for these to be influenced by the presentation of his caste.

He remembered that when, ten years ago, the Triptych System had been formed, an assessment of the power of the System's influence on individual actions, interventions and ideologies had begun. One particularly zealous researcher recorded many thousands of actions, attributing to each of them a figure representing the degree of danger they presented to the stability and security of the Triptych System. Any action exceeding the nine thousand figure was considered dangerous, outlawed and rejected by all the System's electronic memories. The System was thus automatically protected against any dangerous development that might have been overooked by those in charge of security. The modules for this assessment, Kasper now recalled, were named after the researcher who had thought them up, and were known as RMH, "Risk Modules H". Kasper dictated his proposal based on this logic and noted it on his holographic coordinator, to be automatically inserted into his speech as soon as his turn came.

His thoughts ran ahead of those of his teleconference colleagues. The problem was not that certain genetic, android appliances might impose their will on modern, established institutions, but that if for a moment the situation proved beyond the powers of the Controllers of Security, a class of "genetic aristocrats" might materialise and provoke new upheavals and acts of terrorism. The thinking behind his proposal had one central point: those past failures which had marked the early years of the twenty first century must not be repeated. Kasper was adamant about this and highlighted some of these failures, despite the fact that the Triptych System's official policy disapproved of referring to failure. Indeed, there was an effort to airbrush from history many details of the past decades. Details such as the compulsory classification of citizens, the camps, the exiles, the sudden population reductions, the seizure of natural resources from less developed nations by the richer and more powerful, the atrocities committed by fanatics, and more. If any of these were to reoccur, they might trigger major unrest, perhaps catastrophe, since even the front line of defence – the defenders – could not hold back waves of desperate people. Neither the chemical lasers nor the batches of ionized gas at their disposal – among other weapons – could be more efficient than fear and methodical conditioning for effectively controlling the citizen in today's world. Kasper believed that science, instead of seeking to create super-human beings, should instead be strengthening the technology for cerebrally implanting "democratisation", meaning mildness and weakness of resistance.

This was in Kasper's mind when, among other messages on the holograph, one revealed that the defenders had brought in Michos for the examination that he himself had requested.

• • •

The environment Michos found himself in was unexpected. Instead of an interrogation room, this was the central viewing point of a true panorama. Without wishing to, he stared with admiration at the view of almost the whole Mediterranean through the telescopic window panes. A region that for centuries had constituted the known civilized world was now simply an area that constituted a single field of vision and could be controlled by just one person. The man now before him, seated in a revolving chair, a handsome Northern European with features that hinted at rare intellectual qualities.

"As you can see the System has one primary concern, the happiness of the individual." Kasper quickly understood the impression his office had made on Michos, and he wanted to immediately remove any disposition his prisoner might have to distrust him. "This is why the System exists, why I am here, why those defenders who brought you to me gave you a rough time, not really so rough as you must admit. My duty is to discover exactly why you are trying to undermine it. The System, I mean. A system which was established for the protection and wellbeing of every citizen and the whole of society, as well as your own."

Michos' first, positive, impression had gone. This was helped by the unexpected introduction of the man sitting nonchalantly before him, who now gestured to him to sit.

"I forgot to introduce myself," added Kasper the moment Michos sat down. "My name is Kasper and I am in charge of Security for the Eastern Mediterranean and the Middle East. Just before you arrived, I found myself wondering why you made this, needless to say, futile effort to harm the System, knowing as we do that it produces only good results for society."

"You know me. I don't have to introduce myself since it was you who brought me here from so far away," answered Michos mechanically. "What are these good results for society, may I ask?" he continued without hesitation. The game was over. No one was able to prejudge the result but nor was it possible to reverse it if it turned out as he feared. Besides, Kasper's phrase "futile effort" indicated what, from the outset, he and his associates had feared: that they had no hope of success and that their mission was always destined to fail.

"That was precisely the good outcome I was imagining just before you entered my office," remarked Kasper. He was clearly dealing with a persistent man here and he determined to discover everything about him and his co-conspirators. "Since the establishment of the T.S., wealth production on a global scale has increased by 80%. Don't you consider that quite a feat, since it was achieved without the shedding of a single drop of blood? By contrast with the past, when every day brought violent clashes and victims of terrorism?"

"Who has been enriched by the production of wealth? Is it fairly distributed? Or do the rich perhaps become richer while the poor are forced to work not ten days with one day's rest but fifteen consecutive days?" This expedient of the next reform was already being discussed and was not an invention of the moment. There was nothing holding Michos back now. The "perfect" man of power before him was going to hear what he deserved to hear, and Michos did not intend to spare him the details.

"Paradises do not exist in this life." Kasper had decided to make an additional effort to convince his interlocutor. He saw clearly that it would be worth the effort. "Paradises were invented for shirkers. I, in my position, work without the eleventh day of rest that all other citizens including yourself receive. And they were invented not only to keep the shirkers happy but also to deter them from rebellion. Because rebellion demands an effort that might change Paradise, although we must remember that if paradises change they cannot, by definition, change for the better. Only for the worse."

"If human nature were different," answered Michos, "If we did not have an innate thirst for unlimited wealth, if therefore the few did not exercise repressive and inhuman power over the many, if they did not strive by every means to appropriate the goods of the weak person fortunate to be blessed with them, in other words if people were perfect, then perhaps there would be no need for revolutions. Human nature however is different and revolutions are necessary. If, that is, a man does not abandon his fate to the mercy of grasping leaders and his country to mass extermination."

"I believe that your ideas are unfair and mistimed and that you had better consider your defence of the attempt, likely to be judged illegal, to undermine the legal authority. You forget that salary levels were decided after the 2060 nuclear catastrophe in Asia. And that if the analogy of the three categories of citizens, 100 credit units for C, 1000 for B and 10,000 for those in A had not been institutionalized, it would have been impossible for the international economy to survive."

"And the result," persisted Michos, "was for the control of political life to pass into the hands of a small number of plutocrats. Into the hands of those who stood to gain most and who are striving to gain still more. A certain wise leader early in the century said – and I always keep it in mind as a guide – the words: European culture is the product of the parallel action of two elements: the free economy and social solidarity. All of us Europeans have paid a very high price for every attempt to do away with this parallel. And now, I wish to add, it has been paid for by the entire world under the Triptych System, which has thrown the free economy aside and done away with social solidarity."

"What did you and your collaborators hope to achieve?" This time the tone of Kasper's question was less friendly.

"To deal a blow to supranational totalitarianism. To awaken society and make it think again about the principles of our culture which have been taken away. School books have been removed and replaced by snippets of knowledge which encourage the brain to complacency and submission. To resist the elimination of personality and autonomous thinking. Our attempt was a revolution, not violent but cerebral, not of the masses but of the few. For the common good."

"And you were hoping to achieve all this through some form of educative hypnosis, if I correctly understood your female collaborator's explanation? Against her will of course, I have to add."

Michos did not reply as his thoughts dwelt on his ignorance of Amsey's fate. His mind shuddered at the question, "Will I see her again?"

"She told us that you named the procedure 'Accumulative-Monographic Tele-Education' and that within it you concentrated all the relevant classical and modern wisdom relating to the management of society and social justice. Regardless of how much knowledge you were putting into the minds of our fellow citizens, don't you think that the attempt has a certain inexcusable naivety, a certain – perhaps I should say – puerility?"

Michos' silence encouraged Kasper to continue to drive home the futility of this or any attempt, regardless of its nature, to shake an unassailable system such as the Triptych. The Triptych had indeed been planned more than a hundred years ago, at the time of the Third Reich. The organization of a new systemic elite, then called the "Master Plan East". The plan was for an elite to administer, politically and financially, a post-war united Europe. The decision to revive the idea followed the break-up of the European Union and the conflicts plaguing the continent in mid-century.

"With your 'little game', were you seriously hoping to shake a system which had secured so many benefits for the people?" he continued. "A world where the word 'absent-mindedness' no longer exists because there is now an electronic system to remind you of what you should be doing? A world where anyone can speak on the electronic network and instantly learn about whatever appeals to his interest? A world where photovoltaic technology is so universal that no corner of any city is without light at night? A world where genetic maps available to all prepare the citizen for every possible predisposition to health problems? What more can I say to convince you that your entire effort was childish and naïve.....?"

"Within the System, words have evolved to mean the opposite of what they once meant," Michos could not stop himself from saying. "Those with an opposing view no longer have a view. Those who must be kept silent have no need to be muzzled because for many years now the fostering of culture has been so downgraded that criticism is impossible. Everything must appear acceptable, in principle and without question. That is not democracy and when we do not have democracy we cease to be free. And that is unacceptable to one who wishes to be called free. 'If freedom and equality are born in the thoughts of a person, in practice they can only be found in Democracy where all people have the same responsibility for common affairs', says Aristotle." Following this, Michos promised himself to discontinue the discussion. Decisions concerning himself and his collaborators must already have been taken and all he need do now was resign himself to the fate chosen for him by the authorities. His attempt to change the world had clearly failed. He wondered how he could have hoped for anything else. As if to confirm his thoughts, Kasper's next words were:

"You know that our society has a defence system. It has to have. The philosophy behind the T.S. was based, from the beginning, on certain assumptions. Assumptions, and not, as you prefer, principles. Principles cannot secure the smooth operation of a system as complex as ours. There are thus thousands of thoughts that threaten the System, ideas and proposals that go completely against the assumptions. They are classified by category and are automatically controlled by the defence system. We call it the RMH, or Risk Modules H. When such ideas, or principles as you prefer, are disseminated electronically, they are monitored automatically to assess their risk factor for the System; if the factor exceeds a certain level their dissemination is blocked, without the necessity for human intervention. This is what happened with what you called Accumulative Monographic Tele-Education. And simply the word 'accumulative' was enough to raise the alarm."

With these words the meeting drew to a close. Kasper gestured to the defenders that Michos should be temporarily held until the other members of his team were found. He now had to complete his report of the incident.

• • •

The blue shadow passed repeatedly before him. He saw it over and over again and each time he had the impression that he saw something different in the look directed at him, as if Klara were asking something else from him. Hassan had lost all sense of time. If he was asked how long it was since they had left him alone in the room to make the requested changes to his "Logic" card, he could not have said whether it was hours or years. The only thing filling his senses was the shadow of her spirit. The blue shadow ascending quickly into the afterlife with that gesture suggestive of pleading. He felt that little by little he was losing his mind. At any moment the defenders would return and demand why he was delaying carrying out their simple order: to transfer the additional data from the gold card to the bronze one he would from now on own. He thought he heard a noise outside and wondered whether perhaps the pleading look from Klara's spirit had something to do with the task the defenders had given him. Otherwise, what could his beloved possibly expect from him, now that he was to be stripped of every power provided by his special social status. Like a sudden flash of lightning the thought of his vital research work providing invaluable services to the Triptych System came to mind. The ranking of citizens into different categories, such as their average income, likelihood of finding employment, religion - which played an important role in each personal history, from someone's great grandfather down to the time of the research - , beliefs and family attachment to the notion of democracy, and many other categories. He had also recorded all the grades of risk that personal opinions, philosophical ideas and outdated principles posed for the predominance of the Triptych System, in what were called risk modules and named after him: Risk Modules Hassan. And it was these that acted to block any attempt to alter the foundations on which the T.S. stood. And there within him shone the light of the answer he was seeking. The answer to the plea made by Klara's spirit as she left this world forever. She had asked him to do something to subvert the huge wrong done to her, using precisely the means that he had created for the System's protection. But to use it against the System. He knew now what he had to do. Provided he had enough time. If it had not functioned definitely and irreversibly what, for practical reasons, he himself had called "the ideological barrier", and better known as the R.M.H.

He snatched up the gold card and hurried to give one final command.

· · ·

It was midnight when Kasper finished his report for the T.S. He had finally decided that only one interpretation, that of paranoia, would be considered credible by those who viewed these human problems from afar, that is, by the real leaders. Thus his report concluded that the evidence from the recording of the conversation with Michos contained strong indications that all his actions over the past days were the result of a "dangerous paranoid obsession" necessitating his confinement in an appropriate institution.

As the holographic conference with colleagues from the other security departments was coming to an end, he noticed a new item of more direct concern to him. The hologram informed him that the individual charged with neglecting to protect his gold "Logic" card, Hassan Porter, had committed suicide. Only two floors below the office of the Controller for Security in Eastern Europe and the Middle East. Just below his feet.

Kasper gave a long-suffering sigh. Even his improved bio-technological endurance was beginning to let him down. He would have to immediately investigate the complete background of this man who had just taken his own life and make an in-depth check of the action or negligence for which he had been charged, as well as find out how he had managed to escape the attentions of the defenders to carry out the suicide.

Who was Hassan Porter? As Kasper's research progressed, he discovered that he had contributed his extensive capabilities to support for the Triptych System. Kasper also discovered new reasons to worry that the death occurring within the building which was his power base might be far more significant than he had first thought. Then he came across the description of the Risk Modules and he saw that their creation was attributed to Hassan Porter, and that the "H" had been added to honour their creator. Hassan Porter. What followed was the unavoidable question arrived at by Kasper with, it is true to say, considerable misgiving. Had the relevant Risk Modules blocking mechanism managed to function before the suicide of their creator, or not? The block was certainly working. But indications showed that it had ceased to function just seconds before the suicide.

Kasper began another, more complicated and exacting procedure. How much time had elapsed between the Accumulative Monographic Tele-Education of Michos and his collaborators and the cancellation of the "block" by Hassan Porter? Had the new data from Michos' team been neutralized in time by the "block" or not, before it was disabled by its creator? He remembered from past projects that there was a "window of opportunity" before a new item of information became embedded and could replace potentially opposing memories. In the past, this time was estimated at six hours. But technology had a habit, for better or worse, of self-improvement and producing new parameters of its own accord. He decided to dedicate the rest of the night to ascertaining exactly what had happened and whether it was still possible to stop a process that might end up by shaking the very foundations of the System.

• • •

11
FREEDAY

Vlado's gaze had remained fixed on the hologram for several seconds after the end of the broadcast. It was not just the content of the news that he had just heard, even though it was directly related to his own future and that of his fellow inmates at the Purification Camp. It was not just the news that had amazed him, it was the spirit in which it had been announced. A spirit of moderation and almost, he would have said, humanity which rarely characterized the "Central of Holographic Information". A form of information so cold and dry that you would easily have said it had been prepared mechanically and was directed also at soulless beings. Today's information however was different.

Vlado got up and went off in the direction of the living quarters where his new friends lived. From the beginning, he had taken to Nora's family, he had great respect for the profound knowledge of her companion, Kamel and he wanted to be the first to share the good news with them.

"Our journey has probably been postponed," he announced, very discreetly so it did not become a subject for general comment between all their inmates.

"What journey?" asked Kamel mechanically, still half asleep.

"I'm speaking about THE journey. To Mars, of course."

"What makes you say that?"

"It's official information. From C.H.I." All the family had got out of bed. The children raised their eyebrows as if the news was bad; the adults were hankering after more information.

"The news is that the 'Persephone' Programme for the colonization of the planet Mars had a serious problem. There has been, as it said, a discovery by various scientific organizations of a certain mistake in the plans that could prove decisive. The curious thing is that up to now, this discovery was not revealed and I wonder what has happened for it to be revealed at this moment when they are preparing us for the journey. In short, the scientists found that the first settlers would not have survived on the surface of the planet, but not for the reasons that the average citizen might imagine. The scientists believe that the over-production of oxygen that the plants would produce would be the cause of the settlers' death. Given that they would be obliged to cultivate and grow the plants inside the constructions where they themselves are living, the production of oxygen and its diffusion into the environment would be excessive. Because there is as yet no technology that would allow for the removal of excessive oxygen and leave the nitrogen, which is essential for maintaining atmospheric pressure. Besides, the settlers would have to live in a sort of greenhouse with intolerable levels of humidity. The news concluded that under the present conditions and until solutions can be found to the problems of the programme, 'Persephone' would probably be postponed."

"But they have repeatedly assured people that all technical problem have been solved," wondered Kamel, who was not ready to accept a piece of news as unexpected as it was pleasant.

"Yes!Yes!" Marios butted in having just woken up from a wonderful dream in which he was wandering happily around the heavenly landscape.

"The technical problems perhaps have been solved. But they forgot that apart from those there will be people involved who have to have the prerequisites of life they have on Earth. A small detail." Vlado smiled. "A small detail that makes the difference between settlers on Mars living or dying."

"So you believe that our journey has been postponed?" Nora could not believe the change that this news meant for her family.

"Exactly. And something more that made me personally even more happy." Vlado could not contain his enthusiasm. "Tito and Titi who on each morning holographic broadcast have bombarded us with the advantages for society of the journey and the happiness that would fill the hearts of every traveller, did not do us the honour of appearing today. Since it was those two characters who were the main advertisers of the 'Persephone' venture, you can see that their disappearance from the programme is particularly significant."

Kamel listened to Vlado's news with joy but also a certain distrust. "Perhaps," he thought, "The difficulties that had appeared for the whole 'Persephone' project were short-term setbacks and the changes emerging had no connection with conspiratorial intervention of Michos and his team." He had to try and cross-check with someone else from the team. He thought of contacting Michos. Their agreement of course had not favoured this move. Before they split up, they had agreed not to communicate for a time since these contacts would facilitate the Security of the System in tracking them down. The recent development however justified the need for contact to be made between them and perhaps ascertain that their endeavor had, contrary to expectations, turned out to be successful. However, Michos did not respond and Kamel concluded that he had probably fallen into the hands of Security and that lines of communication were dead.

His next move was to communicate with Babar. It was Su who responded to his message. Her voice was strangely different. Kamel cautiously asked how she was.

"Wonderful!" replied Su with almost unnatural enthusiasm, "Both me and Babar."

Kamel remained silent. Su indeed sounded different from the woman he had left only a few hours ago.

"We both had a very pleasant awakening today," Su added. "I wish you to always have a pleasant awakening," said Kamel awkwardly.

"It's not what you think!" Su laughed. "Because today we woke up to different circumstances. We woke up with our heads full of music... music that you know." She added.

"You're not saying..." Kamel's amazement was complete and catalytic.

"I'm telling you. It was 'Joy'. It was Bach! That's what told us that the attempt paid off. Whatever I log onto, the holograms are dominated by the same music. We've won I tell you!"

THE LINCHPIN OF SANITY

The endless plain, as far as the eye could see, the precipice below his feet, the morning breeze and rocky crags around him were, as on other days, his only companions. With a cup in his hand, he was deliberating whether he should drink the beverage prepared for him. He knew that both the food and drink, together with his sleep, were responsible for the change he had noticed in himself over the last days. The compulsory tele-education the System had subjected him to while asleep at night, as well as throughout the day, would gradually produce the results his captors wished for: the neutralizing of all desire and ability to resist the System. It would transform him into a mindless puppet ready to accept any external suggestion without question. The first indication that something was happening to him while asleep occurred on the second day of his detention at the old monastery, when he began to feel unsure about exactly how long he had been imprisoned. Thanks to his pharmaceutical experience, he understood he had to react to this immediately if he wanted to continue thinking rationally. He glanced at the rock beside him that served as part of the wall round the monastery. "One, two, three....eight marks. I've been here for eight days," thought Michos, and he pushed his finger into the gap between the planks nailed together to form the table-top. He pulled out a small nail that he had christened "the linchpin of sanity".

This was the instrument with which he was trying to keep his brain alive. With the nail he scratched one more line next to the other eight. "I am now on the ninth day," he thought with satisfaction and returned the linchpin of sanity to its place between the planks. He had chosen this method for keeping track of time on only the second day. He knew that a correct sense of time was essential for preserving his remaining mental faculties. He discovered the small nail to help count the days, a small nail thus elevated to the status of an intellectual tool of the utmost importance.

The monastery had been renowned in the past principally because the height of its location made it so inaccessible. It had been built many centuries ago, together with several others, on the summits of sheer pillars of rock in the middle of the plain. The area was known as Meteora. In the twentieth century, a hoist attached to a large basket would lift a visiting monk or pilgrim perpendicularly scores of metres to the refectory of the Monastery. Later, before the mid-twenty first century, the Monastery was occupied by fanatical jihadists, who made it their fortress and a look-out post over the surrounding region. The monks just managed to escape in time. Then the Triptych System took over and eradicated all instances of religious fanaticism. From that time on, the Monastery was a place for the confinement and reform of those considered especially dangerous to the System.

Time did not pass quickly. "That's natural," thought Michos. "No prisoner is happy with his situation and because of his impatience to be free again he feels that the hours and days are endless." But he had the linchpin of sanity. He depended upon it and scratched the passing days on the wall with a sense that by so doing he was defeating the System and its plans for him. Until the day when, instead of the green plain beneath the rocks, he saw the whole landscape white with snow. The trees, paths and slopes like fresh brides preparing for life's great journey. He counted the marks on the wall and found only fifteen.

This was puzzling because, from what he remembered when they had brought him here from the last place - he was not sure where that had been - Autumn was just beginning. But the snow quickly melted to reveal the fresh green of the countryside below the narrow iron bars of his window. And the marks on the wall numbered only twenty two. He had completely forgotten why he was in this room day and night and why he was not allowed to go outside. He tried to protest to the guard who brought his food but he paid no attention. When Michos counted the marks he found there were twenty five and from that time on the number remained the same. But it was now impossible for him to understand why he still needed to count that number of twenty five on the wall to remember. And in the morning he forgot to scratch a new mark. Nor did he remember to search for and find his linchpin of sanity.

When the landscape below his window was again covered with snow, the number of markings had not changed and neither did he think of counting them. He now knew that nothing would change and that the linchpin of sanity was no longer there to protect him. It was precisely then, as if the day was predetermined, as if the result of his imprisonment was predetermined, that a guard opened the cell door and informed him that he was free to leave the monastery.

Holding a worker's overalls and a plastic identity card, he found himself in the town close to the monastery. He knew his name. He was called Michos Diakakis, but that was all he knew. The identity card held a number of credit units that would cover his bare essentials. He entered a shop with "Travel Office" written above it and asked to go to the capital, at the same time needing to verify two matters. Firstly, how much money was represented by the numbers on his card, and secondly, which capital was it that he was asking to go to?

Athens was his destination. "But was it?" he wondered. What was he looking for there? There or anywhere else? As he sat in a café, having ordered something to eat and drink, he tried to figure out the answer.

His name was Michos Diakakis. Yes, but what about everything else he should know? He felt so weary, he wished he could return to his cell in Meteora. He wondered where he could find someone to help. So many people around him. Preoccupied with their work. Who could he stop and, most important of all, what could he ask? If he said that he could not remember where he was from and where it was he wanted to go, what would people think of him?

He walked the whole day down a long avenue, trying to remember, until he reached a harbor. He sat on a bench and began to watch the people getting on and off boats. He got up and began to read the names of the ports they were sailing to. And suddenly he read a name, one name, the only one he remembered. He decided there and then to take the ship bound for the only destination that still remained in his dying memory.

. . .

Amsey had found shelter in Ion's sewer for the first three months following her release. There she had tried to hide the pain of her interrogation. She had struggled to forget the remorse that she felt. Remorse for the death of her friend, Klara. She was to blame for Klara's death. Down in the sewer she had tried to hide not only her self-reproach but also her physical self. The implanted tracking device, which the Triptych System had forced on her would not be easy to remove, even by an experienced surgeon in a specially authorized surgery. She continued to try to find someone with experience, however, and above all someone willing to accept the risks involved in removing the device, since such an operation could be highly dangerous. Precautions taken by the System to prevent such illegal operations were highly effective. Finally, a former chemist who had himself ended up in the sewers to avoid the defenders, accepted the task and managed to extract the tracker-microchip. Amsey wanted to leave the sewer but, at the same time, remain invisible to the System in order to be free to find out what had happened to Michos. She took a decision that she would not go back on. Either she found him or that would be the end of her. A certain wise man, possibly Goethe, she was not certain, had written, "Only through love is there immortality." And this had become her mantra.

When, however, after months of confinement in the sewer and the removal of the tracker, she found herself again above ground, she noticed that many changes had taken place. People appeared less afraid, the defenders had disappeared, and work had become more humane. She cautiously asked several people who seemed to her honest and trustworthy what had happened and was given the Proclamation that had apparently circulated soon after her voluntary exile in the sewer. As she read it, an enthusiasm that she had not felt for many years welled up inside her.

PROCLAMATION

Today, on the thirty second day of the eighth month of the year 2071, an emergency meeting of the Three Highest Bodies of the Triptych System was convened and agreement reached on the following:

because the global economy has, after much effort and sacrifices by citizens, returned to satisfactory rhythms;

because social law and order in society has been restored following the terrorist upheavals of the past decades and

because the demographic rate of population increase has reached a controllable level

the Three Highest Bodies of the Triptych System feel it appropriate to urgently examine the possibility of realizing and immediately implementing the following reforms:

-The state banks shall henceforth provide loans to households at 1% interest.

- A home shall henceforth be considered an inalienable human right. No citizen can be deprived of it.

-Newly-wed couples shall henceforth receive a marriage subsidy of 20,000 credit units from the Triptych System.

-Henceforth, education and medical treatment shall be free of charge for all.

-All citizens deciding to follow professions in agriculture shall receive land, free housing and free equipment to establish their farms.

-If a citizen on just grounds cannot find employment after completing his/her education, the Triptych System shall provide half the salary earned if the citizen were in his/her chosen employment until employment is found.

- The present salary scale shall cease to exist and henceforth the three salary scales of 100, 250 and 400 credit units are now in force (instead of 100, 1.000 and 10.000).

- Work is about to begin on the reintroduction of the calendar and working hours based on the seven-day week and one or two non- working days a week. In addition, the twelve-month year will be reintroduced....

• • •

The more Amsey read, the more she felt an unprecedented wave of joy rising inside her. It was obvious that all the effort and sacrifices of Michos' team had not been in vain. All this could not be simply a coincidence. And from all the references in the latter part of the text it seemed that the changes had greater scope than appeared at first glance. That they related to a huge number of citizens and would radically change their lives for the better and bring about a fairer distribution of wealth. From that moment began Amsey's tireless effort to find Michos. It was not only a matter of finding the man she loved; the only man with whom she had found true tenderness and warmth. It was also that he had brought off an incredible feat, a humanitarian achievement that very few in history could boast of accomplishing. However, the days and weeks passed with no result. No authority was in a position to provide her with useful information. "He was confined either in a prison or in a Purification camp somewhere," thought Amsey. "But most of the detainees accused of dangerous activities against the regime had been released and the ones still incarcerated had had nothing to do with such activities."

The months passed and there came a point when Amsey became tired of seeing no result for her efforts. It was strange that with all the means society now had at its disposal in the field of communications - electronic, holographic and telecommunications – it was impossible to ascertain whether a person was alive or dead. And if alive, precisely where he was. At the end of the first year following her departure from the sewers, she decided to create a search base from a specific location and continue looking for him from there. In any case, the credit units she had saved were beginning to run out and the cost of her many journeys had limited her opportunities.

Conan was an unexpected joy for Amsey, shortly after she set up home in the tourist cabin of the Petrified Forest on Mytilene where she had last seen Michos. Amsey remembered him as one of four identical wolfhounds, the "guard dogs" that Klara had created for her by the method of cloning. She had sent it to the vet for vaccination just a few hours before the defenders invaded her floating residence. Conan threw himself at her and showed his own joy by rubbing his nose against her cheek. "From the happy, old gang we are the only two left," murmured Amsey. "You'll stay with me, to remind me of Klara."

• • •

"To the Petrified Forest." He read the sign at the side of the road. It was as if the strange name reminded him of something. "Imagine there being a forest with trees of stone…a forest of trees with no sap… There's another image that reminds me of something…What did some people used to say about the sap that trees have in their trunks? Ah! Yes! They used to say that the sap inside trees carries human memories or something like that. But these trees outside the town don't have sap, so they can't have memories. They are fossilized, like me, without memories, without sap. Made of stone."

Michos remained thinking for a moment, and then, "Perhaps I should go and see if they look like me. To make sure I am as dead as they are!" He laughed.

• • •

It was Spring once again. The time when Amsey's whole being was revitalised. Putting behind her any vestige of winter time melancholy. The annual visit to the vet for Conan's vaccination had given Amsey the opportunity to revisit the island's capital. Mytilene's waterfront shone with the reflections of the sunny promenade alongside it. Conan ran up and down trying to find a cat to chase, or at least a duck that might have taken the risk of walking among the pedestrians. Conan stopped and suddenly retraced his steps. To take another look and sniff at the wretched beggar. He looked like a beggar, dressed in tattered worker's overalls, all skin and bone and a long beard, sitting on the steps of the harbour police building, with blank eyes and an even blanker expression, as if he had been waiting a lifetime for something to appear out of the sea. Conan approached and cocked his head on one side, as dogs do when something puzzles them. He returned to Amsey's side. Looking now at her, he cocked his head on one side again and wagged his tail, perplexed that she should not recognize her beloved. He went back and showed him to her with a movement of the head. She followed Conan.

And Michos, behind his thick beard and bushy eyebrows, suddenly saw the beautiful woman recognize him and burst into tears.

• • •

www.ingramcontent.com/pod-product-compliance
Lightning Source LLC
Chambersburg PA
CBHW070654290526
45790CB00001B/310